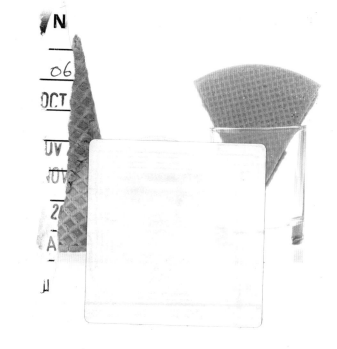

just desserts

daniel tay

APPLE

First published in the UK in 2008 by
Apple Press
7 Greenland Street
London NW1 0ND
United Kingdom
www.apple-press.com

ISBN: 978-1-84543-269-0

Editor : Sylvy Soh
Designer : Lynn Chin Nyuk Ling
Photographer : Joshua Tan, Elements By The Box

Published by Marshall Cavendish Cuisine
An imprint of Marshall Cavendish International
1 New Industrial Road, Singapore 536196

Other Marshall Cavendish Offices:
Marshall Cavendish Ltd. 119 Wardour Street, London W1F 0UW, UK
• Marshall Cavendish Corporation. 99 White Plains Road, Tarrytown NY
10591-9001, USA • Marshall Cavendish International (Thailand)
Co Ltd. 253 Asoke, 12th Flr, Sukhumvit 21 Road, Klongtoey Nua,
Wattana, Bangkok 10110, Thailand • Marshall Cavendish (Malaysia)
Sdn Bhd, Times Subang, Lot 46, Subang Hi-Tech Industrial Park,
Batu Tiga, 40000 Shah Alam, Selangor Darul Ehsan, Malaysia

Marshall Cavendish is a trademark of Times Publishing Limited

Printed in Singapore by KWF Printing Pte Ltd

To my staff,
who have been with me
throughout these years.
Thank you for trusting
my vision and allowing me
to lead you.

To my wife, thank you for
your understanding
and patience.

{ contents }

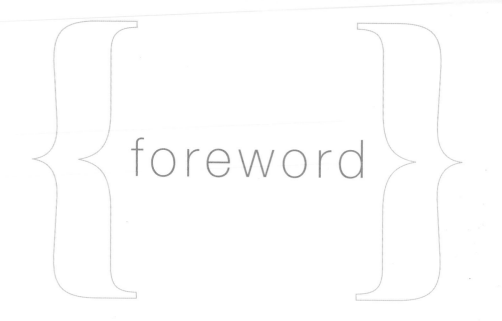

{ foreword }

I have known Daniel Tay since his snooker-loving days.
His father owned a bakery at that time and had a hidden desire
for Daniel to succeed his business eventually. There was,
however, not the slightest hint of interest on Daniel's part to
be involved in the bakery business. After much persuasion, his
father managed to convince him to enrol for a baking course,
to get him away from the snooker table.

I was Daniel's instructor for a six-week baking course at the UFM Baking and Cooking School in Bangkok, Thailand. His father's plan to get him away from the snooker table failed, for Daniel brought along his cue, spent the nights playing, and ended up sleeping in my classes the following day. I confronted him and told him that there was nothing wrong with playing snooker, just that he had to play it well enough to be a professional, so he would be able to earn his own keep and not be a burden to his family or to society. Failing that, the alternative was to get into the food trade, where at least he would never be hungry! Thankfully, I managed to convince him that baking was a profession he could excel in and be proud of.

To me, a baker is both an artist and a scientist. As an artist, the baker needs to be creative in making desserts, cakes and pastries into forms and shapes that are appealing to the eye. As a scientist, he has

to have knowledge in chemistry, biology and physics in order to create and maintain the best flavour and colour for his products on a daily basis, despite factors such as changes in the ingredients and unstable environmental conditions.

Daniel's turning point came about when he dedicated himself to the task of learning how to create the best products possible. He continues to work with passion today, and has not compromised on quality. He remembers his humble beginnings and, based on his experience, encourages his staff to obtain proper baking qualifications and work professionally and diligently. His hard work over the years has indeed paid off, and I am proud to be his first mentor.

Thank you, Daniel, for sharing your knowledge with us and producing a book that both professionals and beginners alike can use as a reference.

Roy Chung
Bakery Consultant
US Wheat Associates Singapore

{ introduction }

My baking philosophy stems from my belief in the importance of the taste and texture of the final product, with presentation taking a supporting role. For instance, a well-executed soufflé or crème brûlée on its own, without any superfluous garnishing, can taste amazing. They are simple creations, yet have survived over the years as timeless desserts. It is the basics of such simple yet enjoyable recipes, that I aim to share in this cookbook.

One book that has never failed to inspire me to bake (and cook) is *Chez Panisse Cooking* by Alice Waters. There are no photos to illustrate the recipes—just straightforward descriptions and information on how the renowned Alice Waters sources for the best and freshest ingredients and prepares them. She demonstrates that food doesn't have to be fancy to be delicious. For example, her definition of a dessert can be a mere bowl of fresh fruits from selected farms in California. Sans impractical decoration or styling, pure simplicity, if executed in the right manner, can create a wonderful dish or dessert.

I have adhered to this same philosophy throughout my career as a pastry chef and in working on this cookbook. From a rustic, crusty Country Bread and a thick, hearty Waffle, to a no-frills Chocolate Crunch Cake, a fragrant Cinnamon Ice Cream and a warming Ginger Milk Pudding, the recipes I have chosen to feature here in *Just Desserts* are simple and unpretentious. The taste and texture of each of these creations speak for themselves.

In mulling over an appropriate title for this book, my editors and I finally decided on *Just Desserts*, as it encompasses the very philosophy that runs throughout this book. These are literally just desserts—honest and true, yet everything that a dessert should be.

Follow these recipes to create the basic desserts, then present them as you wish. Take special care when measuring out the ingredients however, as it is very important for bakers to be precise. The measurements will determine the final character of the baked good. For example, in making bread, adding too much salt will alter the timing for dough fermentation and cause the yeast function to be less active, resulting in bread that does not rise satisfactorily.

With this book, I hope to encourage home cooks who enjoy baking as a hobby, young, aspiring chefs, or even professional bakers who feel that my baking tips will work for them. My advice is to be patient, to practise and learn, as well as to throw in a good dose of passion to perfect your baking skills.

Daniel Tay

{ kitchen

equipment

It is important to select the correct baking tools to create the best results, but it is not necessary to invest in terribly pricey equipment. However as the saying goes, "you get what you pay for". For example, a blender with plastic blades might be cheaper and good enough for blending soft foods, but a blender with stainless steel blades will be more effective in breaking down ingredients that are hard in texture, such as certain types of nuts. Bearing in mind that this book is written for the home chef, here is a list of baking utensils essential for getting started.

Electric Mixer A good electric mixer will have variable mixing speeds and come complete with beater, paddle, whisk and dough hook attachments. Choose a mixer that comes with a 5-litre (160-fl oz / 20-cup) mixing bowl, for blending larger quantities.

Handheld Blender A powerful handheld blender is important for blending ingredients until the mixture is homogenous.

Scraper It is handy to have both a stainless-steel bench scraper and a plastic pastry scraper among your baking tools. The bench scraper (a rectangular blade with a grip on one edge) is used for dividing dough into smaller portions or scraping dough off a work surface. Plastic scrapers should be thin and flexible for scraping batter or dough that sticks to the sides of a mixing bowl, to ensure the mixture is well combined, or to remove excess batter.

Thermometer It is important to maintain the correct temperature when baking. A digital thermometer is ideal for checking the temperature of liquids, while a mercury thermometer is perfect for measuring oven heat.

Weighing Scale Choose a digital scale with a resolution of increments measure in grams for accurate measurements.

Whisk This tool is used for incorporating air into a mixture, beating eggs, mixing liquids or whipping creams.

Bain Marie A bain marie is essentially a water bath used for delicate items such as custards, mousses, cheesecakes and puddings that require gentle, moist and insulated heat, to prevent them from cracking, drying out or curdling, as such desserts are prone to under a direct source of dry heat such as the oven. A roasting pan is usually used to hold a smaller pan, ramekin or tray filled with the desired mixture, and hot water is then poured into the larger pan until it reaches about halfway up the smaller dish. Check the water level occasionally when baking and add more hot water if necessary.

Melting Chocolate Melting chocolate requires care as chocolate is sensitive to heat and will become hard, grainy or lumpy if over-heated. This can also happen if liquid or steam comes into contact with the chocolate while it is being melted. Adding butter or oil to the melted chocolate can help make it smoother. Break or chop chocolate into small pieces so that the melting process is faster and the chocolate does not scorch. Place chocolate in a dry heatproof bowl and set it over a pot of gently simmering water. While the chocolate is melting, remove both the pot and bowl from the heat (in case it gets too hot), then gently stir chocolate over the pot of hot water until it melts completely.

Folding This technique combines a light ingredient into a heavier mixture, so that the original volume is maintained. An example is adding whisked egg whites or sifted flour to a cake batter. To do this, use a rubber spatula to fold the mixture (cut vertically through the mixtures, across the bottom, then up and over the top) quickly but gently, and stop as soon as the ingredients are combined.

Whipping This technique incorporates air into an ingredient or mixture, such as egg whites or cream, to increase its volume and make it light and fluffy. This is done by rapidly beating or whipping the mixture in a circular motion using a wire whisk or electric mixer.

techniques }

{ basic recipes }

In the busy world of today, where one is often pressed for time, it is far easier to go to a store and purchase ready-made pastries and creams. However, learning how to prepare these basic recipes from scratch will prove to be extremely fulfilling and become an invaluable skill!

crème patissiere

Makes about 770 g (1 lb 11 oz)

Corn flour (cornstarch) *40 g (1¹/₂ oz)*

Milk *450 ml (15 fl oz / 1⁴/₅ cups)*

Egg yolks *120 g (4 oz)*

Single (light) cream *3¹/₄ Tbsp*

Sugar *100 g (3¹/₂ oz)*

Vanilla bean *1, scraped for seeds and reserve pod, or use 2 tsp vanilla essence*

Unsalted butter *15 g (¹/₂ oz)*

- Place corn flour, 125 ml (4 fl oz / ¹/₂ cup) milk and egg yolks in a mixing bowl and whisk until well blended. Set aside.

- Combine remaining milk, cream and sugar in a pot and bring to the boil. Add vanilla seeds and pod to infuse flavour and stir well.

- Pour half of milk mixture into egg mixture to temper it. Stir constantly, until mixture is smooth and well blended.

- Return mixture to pot and cook over very low heat. Whisk until mixture thickens. Cook for another 5–10 minutes or until mixture is smooth and shiny. Remove from heat and set aside to cool to 45°C (113°F). Whisk in butter until well blended.

- Store in an airtight container and refrigerate until ready to use.

tempered chocolate

Makes about 500 g (1 lb 1¹/₂ oz)

Chocolate *500 g (1 lb 1¹/₂ oz)*

- Melt 350 g (11¹/₂ oz) chocolate in a bain-marie to 45°C (113°F). Stir constantly to prevent burning. Remove from heat and set aside to cool to 30°C (72°F).

- Cut remaining chocolate into fine slivers and add to melted chocolate. Pour onto a marble or granite surface and stir with a spatula until chocolate cools to 27°C (80°F). Use immediately.

From left: Chocolate shapes made from tempered chocolate; Crème Patissiere

almond cream

Makes about 840 g (1⁴/₅ lb)

Single (light) cream *125 ml (4 fl oz / ¹/₂ cup)*

Ground almonds *200 g (7 oz), finely ground*

Corn flour (cornstarch) *20 g (²/₃ oz)*

Unsalted butter *150 g (5¹/₃ oz), softened*

Icing (confectioner's) sugar *200 g (7 oz)*

Eggs *125 g (4¹/₂ oz)*

Rum *1–2 Tbsp*

- If cream has been chilled in the refrigerator, leave to thaw at room temperature for 10 minutes before use.

- Place almonds, corn flour, butter and sugar in a mixing bowl and beat for 10 minutes, or until batter is free from lumps. Add eggs one at a time and stir to blend well. Add cream and rum and stir until smooth.

- Store in an airtight container and refrigerate until ready to use.

levain

Makes about 2 kg (4 lb 6 oz)

Day 1

Bread flour *500 g (1 lb 1¹/₂ oz), sifted*

Water *500 ml (16 fl oz / 2 cups)*

Yeast *a pinch*

Day 2

Bread flour *500 g (1 lb 1¹/₂ oz), sifted*

Water *300 ml (10 fl oz / 1¹/₄ cups)*

Salt *20 g (²/₃ oz)*

Day 3

Bread flour *500 g (1 lb 1¹/₂ oz), sifted*

Water *375 ml (12 fl oz / 1¹/₂ cups)*

Salt *10 g (¹/₃ oz)*

- Start preparations for levain 3 days ahead.

- Combine all ingredients for Day 1 in a mixing bowl and mix well. Knead mixture into a wet and sticky dough, cover and leave to rest in a warm place overnight.

- Combine all ingredients for Day 2 in a mixing bowl and mix well. Add to dough from Day 1 and knead together to combine. Leave to rest in a warm place overnight.

- On Day 3, divide combined dough in half. This recipe requires only one portion of dough. Discard other half. Combine all ingredients for Day 3 in a mixing bowl and mix well. Add portion of combined dough and knead together.

- Leave levain to prove in a warm place until doubled in volume. Cover with plastic wrap and refrigerate until ready to use.

From left: Levain, Almond Cream

lemon cream

Makes about 900 g (2 lb)

Eggs *200 g (7 oz)*

Sugar *240 g (8¹/₂ oz)*

Lemon juice *150 ml (5¹/₃ fl oz / ³/₅ cup)*

Lemon *1, grated for zest*

Unsalted butter *300 g (10¹/₂ oz), softened*

- Place eggs in a mixing bowl and add sugar, lemon juice and zest. Whisk ingredients until well blended.

- Pour mixture into a saucepan and cook over low heat. Stir constantly, until mixture has thickened slightly. Remove from heat, transfer to a mixing bowl and place in an ice bath to cool mixture to 45°C (113°F). Whisk in butter until well blended and smooth.

- Pour cream into an airtight container and refrigerator for at least 4 hours before using.

crumble dough

Makes about 1 kg (2 lb 3 oz)

Unsalted butter *250 g (9 oz)*

Plain (all-purpose) flour *250 g (9 oz)*

Icing (confectioner's) sugar *250 g (9 oz)*

Ground almond *250 g (9 oz)*

- Combine ingredients in an electric mixer with a dough hook and knead into a firm dough. Refrigerate for 1 hour.

- Preheat oven to 180°C (350°F).

- Break chilled dough into small pieces using your hands. Arrange on a baking tray and bake for 15 minutes or until golden brown.

- Leave crumble dough to cool before using, or store in the freezer for up to 2 months.

From left: Crumble Dough, Lemon Cream

puff pastry

Makes about 2 kg (4 lb 6 oz)

roll-in

Plain (all-purpose) flour
280 g (10 oz)

Unsalted butter *700 g
(1¹/₂ lb), softened*

dough

Plain (all-purpose) flour
450 g (1 lb)

Salt *15 g (¹/₂ oz)*

Water *150 ml (5¹/₃ fl oz / ³/₅ cup)*

Crushed ice *150 g (5¹/₃ oz)*

Unsalted butter *65 g (2¹/₃ oz)*

- Prepare roll-in a day ahead.

- Place flour and butter in a mixing bowl and stir until smooth and well blended. Roll mixture out into a rectangular sheet and place on a lined sheet pan. Cover with plastic wrap and refrigerate for at least 15 hours.

- Prepare dough. Combine all ingredients in a mixing bowl and mix on low speed until smooth. Roll out into a sheet twice as long as butter sheet and place on another lined sheet pan.

- Centre chilled roll-in on dough sheet. Fold dough over roll-in, so the ends meet at the centre. Press edges of dough together to seal, then cover with plastic wrap. Place on a sheet pan and return to the refrigerator for 1 hour.

- On a floured work surface, roll dough parcel out into a 0.6-cm (¹/₄-in) thick rectangular sheet. Create a book-fold by folding in far ends of dough to meet at the centre, then folding dough again in half. Dough should have 4 layers altogether. Repeat this procedure 4 times.

- Cover dough with plastic wrap and store in the freezer for up to 6 months. Thaw before use.

meringues

A meringue is essentially egg whites and sugar whipped together.
It can be used as a leavener in sponge cakes and soufflés,
added to cream to lighten it or used as a filling or topping.
Sugar serves to stabilise the foam produced from beating the egg whites.
The method of incorporating the sugar determines the type of meringue
produced. The recipes in this book requires different types of meringue,
and the quantities of egg and sugar differ. Hence the meringue
recipes will be listed with the various recipes that require them.

italian meringue

An Italian meringue requires sugar to be melted
to a certain temperature, then incorporated into
the egg whites through whisking. It is typically
used as a base for butter cream or as a filling.

basic meringue

A basic meringue simply requires egg whites
and sugar to be whisked together into soft,
medium or stiff peaks, according to recipe
requirements. Unlike the egg whites in the
Italian meringue, egg whites in the basic
meringue are not heated to a temperature safe
for consumption. It is therefore advisable to
use the basic meringue only as part of a recipe
application that involves cooking.

butter cream

crème anglaise

Milk *180 ml (6 fl oz / 3/4 cups)*

Sugar *85 g (3 oz)*

Egg yolks *140 g (5 oz)*

Unsalted butter *750 g (1 lb 10 1/2 oz)*

italian meringue

Egg whites *55 g (2 oz)*

Sugar *110 g (4 oz)*

Makes about 1.4 kg (3 lb 4 oz)

- Prepare *crème anglaise*. Combine milk and sugar in a pot and bring to the boil. Beat egg yolks in a mixing bowl, then gradually add milk mixture to temper egg yolks, stirring constantly until smooth and well blended.

- Return mixture to the pot and cook over very low heat, stirring constantly until mixture reaches 85°C (185°F). Remove from heat and whisk in butter.

- Prepare Italian meringue. Place egg whites in a mixing bowl. Heat sugar in a saucepan to 120°C (250°F), then pour into egg whites and beat until meringue is shiny and smooth, with stiff peaks. Fold into *crème anglaise* until fully incorporated.

- Store in an airtight container and refrigerate until ready to use.

sablé dough

Unsalted butter *350 g (12 1/2 oz)*

Plain (all purpose) flour *500 g (1 lb 1 1/2 oz)*

Salt *5 g (1/6 oz)*

Icing (confectioner's) sugar *200 g (7 oz)*

Blanched almonds *70 g (2 1/2 oz), finely ground*

Eggs *110 g (4 oz)*

Makes about 1.2 kg (2 lb 3 1/2 oz)

- Cut butter into small cubes and place in a mixing bowl. Add flour, salt, icing sugar and almonds and blend at medium speed to form a dough. Crack eggs into dough and blend on low speed until smooth.

- Cover dough with plastic wrap and refrigerate for 2–3 hours before using.

From left: Sablé Dough, Butter Cream

{ breads }

The smell of freshly baked bread is often said to be one of life's simplest, yet most pleasurable indulgences. Imagine biting into a flaky, buttery croissant over a cuppa, or filling the entire house with the sweet fragrance of baked country bread that goes perfectly with soups, stews and your favourite homemade jam.

brioche

Makes 2–3 loaves

Bread flour *1 kg (2 lb 3 oz), sifted*
Instant yeast *10 g (¹/₃ oz)*
Salt *30 g (1 oz)*
Sugar *125 g (4¹/₂ oz)*
Milk *100 ml (3¹/₂ fl oz / ²/₅ cup)*
Eggs *480 g (17 oz)*
Unsalted butter *700 g (1¹/₂ lb), at room temperature*

- Start preparations 2 days in advance. Place ingredients in the refrigerator to chill overnight.

- Using an electric mixer fitted with a dough hook, mix chilled flour, yeast, salt and sugar. Gradually add milk and eggs and mix to form a dough. Cut butter into small cubes and add to dough. Mix at medium speed until dough is shiny and smooth.

- Leave dough in the mixing bowl and cover with plastic wrap. Set aside to ferment at about 22°C (71°F) for 2 hours, then refrigerate overnight.

- On a floured work surface, divide dough into 350 g (12¹/₃ oz) portions and shape into smooth, round balls. Place dough balls into lightly oiled or lined brioche moulds and leave to prove at room temperature until doubled in volume.

- Bake in a preheated oven at 180°C (350°F) for 30–35 minutes or until golden brown. Set aside to cool.

- Cut into 2.5-cm (1–in) thick slices and spread with desired topping to serve.

1 Cut and weigh dough into desired portions. 2 Shape dough into smooth, round balls. Dough should be smooth and soft, with a rich yellow colour due to its high egg and butter content. 3 After proving, dough should double in volume until nearly reaching the brim of brioche moulds.

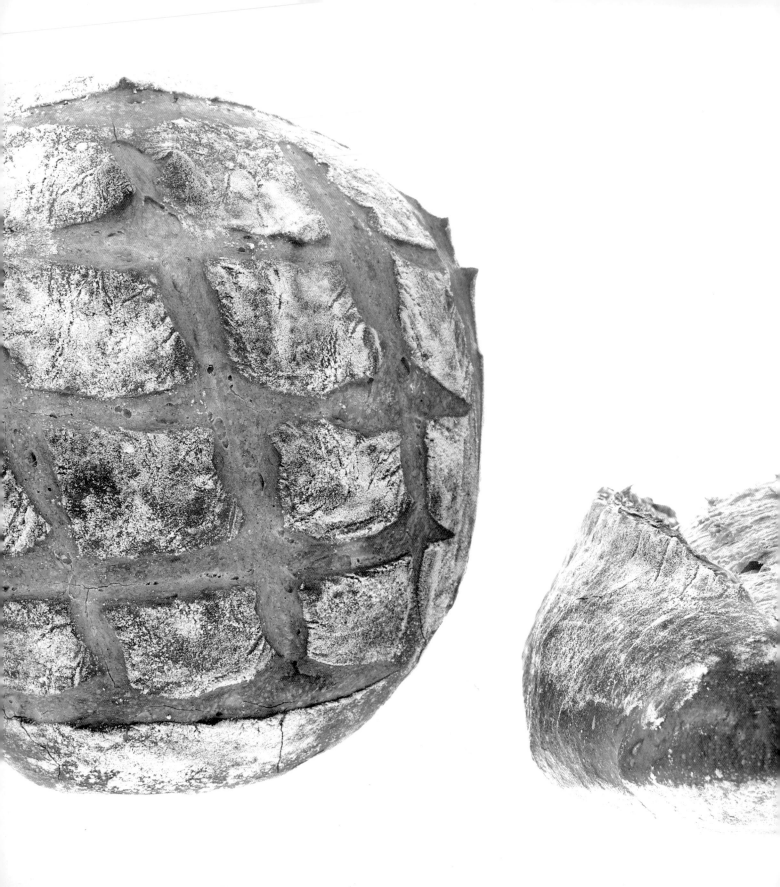

country bread

Makes 4 medium loaves

Bread flour
800 g (1³/₄ lb), sifted

Rye flour *200 g (7 oz), sifted*

Instant yeast *3 g (¹/₈ oz)*

Ice *300 g (10¹/₂ oz), crushed*

Water *350 ml (12¹/₃ fl oz / 1²/₅ cups)*

Levain (page 24) *1 kg (2 lb 3 oz)*

Salt *20 g (²/₃ oz)*

- Using an electric mixer fitted with a dough hook, mix both types of flour and yeast well. Add crushed ice and water and mix on low speed for 3 minutes or until dough is 24°C (75°F). Leave dough to rest for 30 minutes.

- Knead levain and dough together at low speed for 10–15 minutes. Add salt during last 5 minutes of kneading. Dough should be very smooth, soft and slightly elastic.

- Leave dough in the mixing bowl and seal with plastic wrap. Set aside to ferment in a warm, draft-free place for 2 hours.

- Turn dough out on a floured work surface, and fold it over several times to expel any carbon dioxide generated during proofing.

- Using a bench knife, divide dough into 4 portions and shape into smooth, round balls. Cover with plastic wrap and leave to rest for 30 minutes or until doubled in volume.

- Shape dough portions into desired shapes and place on a lined baking tray. Leave to proof in a warm, draft-free place for about 1¹/₂ hours.

- Using a sharp knife, make several cuts on surface of dough for design. Bake in a preheated oven at 250°C (475°F) for 30 minutes or until golden brown. To test for doneness, tap surface of bread. A hollow sound indicates that bread is ready.

1 Knead dough to a soft and smooth consistency. Dough should be slightly elastic and not break easily when lightly pulled. 2 After proving, dough should double in volume. 3 Divide dough into desired portions and shape into smooth, round balls.

croissants

Bread flour *500 g (1 lb 1¹/₂ oz)*
Instant yeast *5 g (¹/₆ oz)*
Bread improver *5 g (¹/₆ oz)*
Sugar *40 g (1¹/₂ oz)*
Salt *10 g (¹/₃ oz)*
Egg *25 g (⁴/₅ oz)*
Milk *200 ml (7 fl oz / ⁴/₅ cup)*
Ice *100 g (3¹/₂ oz)*
Unsalted butter *30 g (1 oz)*
Butter sheet *300 g (10¹/₂ oz), lightly thawed*

egg wash

Egg *30 g (1 oz)*
Milk *1 Tbsp*

- Start preparations 1 day ahead.

- Using an electric mixer fitted with a dough hook, combine flour, yeast, bread improver, sugar and salt in a mixing bowl and mix well. Add egg, milk, ice and unsalted butter and mix on low speed. Increase to medium speed and continue to mix to form a smooth dough. Cover dough with plastic wrap and leave to rest for 1–2 hours, then refrigerate for at least 24 hours.

- On a floured work surface, roll chilled dough out into 1-cm (¹/₂-in) thick sheet, twice as wide as butter sheet. Centre butter sheet on dough sheet. Fold dough over butter sheet, so the ends meet at the centre (see Step 1). On a floured work surface, shift dough parcel so the open ends face to your left and right (see Step 2). Roll dough parcel out to lock butter sheet in.

- Create a book-fold by folding in far ends of dough to meet at the centre, then folding dough again in half. Dough should have 4 layers altogether (see Step 3). Cover with plastic wrap and refrigerate for 20–30 minutes. Repeat this procedure 2 times.

- Roll dough out into a long rectangular sheet about 0.3-cm (¹/₈-in) thick. Cut dough in half along its length.

- Cut out about 20 tall isosceles triangles from dough. Roll each triangle up from its base to the tip, tucking the tip under the croissant (see Step 4). Arrange croissants on a lined baking tray and leave to proof at 28°–30°C (82°–86°F) for 1–2 hours.

- Prepare egg wash. Combine egg and milk and beat lightly. Brush over croissants.

- Bake croissants in a preheated oven at 230°C (450°F) for 20–25 minutes or until golden brown. Remove and leave to cool before serving.

1 Fold dough over butter sheet so the ends meet in the centre. If butter sheet is hard and frozen, leave to thaw a little at room temperature. 2 Turn dough parcel so that the open ends face away from you. Roll out on a floured working surface. 3 Create a book-fold as described in the recipe. 4 Roll each dough triangle up so the tip ends up at the centre and is tucked on the underside of the croissant.

biscuits and pastries

Bite into an éclair filled with luscious chocolate cream that mingles with the melt-in-the-mouth choux pastry. Delight in a tray of golden brown biscotti that goes perfectly with a cup of coffee. Give the kids a sweet surprise with golden brown waffles topped with their favourite ice cream.

canelés

Milk *250 ml (8 fl oz / 1 cup)*

Vanilla bean *1, scraped for seeds and reserve pod, or use 2 tsp vanilla essence*

Unsalted butter *30 g (1 oz)*

Egg yolks *45 g (1¹/₂ oz)*

Egg *25 g (⁴/₅ oz)*

Sugar *225 g (8 oz)*

Plain (all-purpose) flour *125 g (4¹/₂ oz), sifted*

Rum *3 Tbsp*

Beeswax *for coating moulds*

- Start preparations 1 day ahead.

- Combine milk, vanilla seeds and pod or vanilla essence and butter in a pot. Bring to the boil, stirring constantly, until butter is completely melted. Remove pot from heat and discard vanilla pod. Set mixture aside to cool to 85°C (185°F).

- Place egg yolks, egg and sugar in a mixing bowl and whisk until light and pale. Gradually in fold flour, then add cooled milk mixture and mix well. Cover and refrigerate overnight.

- Add rum to refrigerated batter and stir well.

- Coat canalé moulds with beeswax or butter, then fill up to three-quarters full with batter. Bake in a preheated oven at 190°C (370°F) if using small moulds and 150°C (250°F) for large moulds. Bake for 1 hour until crisp and dark brown.

- Serve canelés warm or leave to cool before storing in an airtight container in a cool place for up to 7 days.

éclairs

choux pastry

Butter *100 g (3¹/₂ oz)*

Inverted sugar syrup (trimoline) *5 ml (¹/₆ oz)*

Salt *1 g (¹/₈ oz)*

Water *125 ml (4 fl oz / ¹/₂ cup)*

Milk *150 ml (5 ¹/₃ fl oz / ³/₅ cup)*

Plain (all-purpose) flour *150 g (5¹/₃ oz)*

Eggs *200 g (7 oz)*

Egg yolks *2, beaten, for brushing*

chocolate cream filling

Crème patisserie (page 23) *500 g (1 lb 1¹/₂ oz)*

Dark chocolate *150 g (5¹/₃ oz), finely chopped*

Whipping cream *150 ml (5¹/₃ fl oz / ³/₅ cup)*

Store-bought chocolate glaze or fondant *for glazing*

coffee cream filling

Espresso *60 ml (2 fl oz / ¹/₄ cup)*

Crème patisserie (page 23) *500 g (1 lb 1¹/₂ oz)*

Whipping cream *150 ml (5¹/₃ fl oz / ³/₅ cup)*

Store-bought coffee glaze or fondant *for glazing*

Makes 10–12 éclairs

- Prepare choux pastry. Combine butter, sugar and salt in a mixing bowl and mix well. Transfer to a pot and place over low heat, then add water and 2 Tbsp milk and stir well. Bring mixture to the boil, then gradually add flour, stirring constantly. Stir until dough is formed and leaves side of pot.

- Mix dough at low speed for 5 minutes, then add remaining milk. Gradually add eggs and mix until fully incorporated. Dough should cool to about 42°C (107°F) and be smooth and moist.

- Spoon dough into a piping bag and pipe 14-cm (5¹/₂-in) oblongs, 5-cm (2-in) apart, onto a lined baking tray. Lightly brush with egg yolk and bake at 180°C (350°F) for 45 minutes or until éclairs are puffed and golden brown.

- Make a small hole at one end of each éclair to allow moisture to escape. Set aside to cool.

Chocolate cream éclairs

- Prepare chocolate cream filling. Combine chocolate and crème patisserie and mix well, then fold in whipping cream until fully incorporated.

- Spoon filling into a piping bag and pipe into the small hole made in éclairs. Brush éclairs with chocolate glaze and leave to set before serving. Garnish as desired.

Coffee cream éclairs

- Prepare coffee cream filling. Combine espresso and crème patisserie and mix well, then fold in whipping cream until fully incorporated.

- Spoon filling into a piping bag and pipe into the small hole made in éclairs. Brush éclairs with coffee glaze and leave to set before serving. Garnish as desired.

waffles

Makes 14–16 large waffles

waffles

Plain (all-purpose) flour
400 g (14^1/$_3$ oz), sifted

Baking powder *30 g (1 oz), sifted*

Salt *5 g (^{1}/$_6$ oz)*

Egg yolks *125 g (4^1/$_2$ oz),
at room temperature*

Milk *560 ml (19 fl oz / 2^2/$_5$ cups),
at room temperature*

Unsalted butter
380 g (13^1/$_2$ oz), softened

Cream cheese ice cream
(page 119)

basic meringue for waffles

Egg whites *230 g (8 oz),
at room temperature*

Sugar *45 g (1^1/$_2$ oz)*

strawberry coulis

Strawberry purée *200 ml
(7 fl oz / ^{4}/$_5$ cups)*

Sugar *10 g (^{1}/$_3$ oz)*

Water *2–3 Tbsp*

Lemon juice *5 g (^{1}/$_6$ oz)*

Strawberries *40 g (1^1/$_2$ oz), frozen*

- Prepare strawberry coulis. Combine strawberry purée, sugar and water in a pot and bring to the boil. Stir constantly until sugar is completely dissolved. Set aside to cool. Add lemon juice and strawberries and stir well. Refrigerate until ready to use.

- Prepare waffles. Combine flour, baking powder and salt in a mixing bowl. Mix well and set aside.

- Place egg yolks in another mixing bowl and whisk until foamy, then add milk and continue to whisk until light and fluffy. Add to flour mixture and mix until well blended.

- Melt butter in a pot until temperature is 50°C (122°F). Gradually add to batter and mix well. Set aside.

- Prepare basic meringue. Whisk egg whites in a mixing bowl until foamy. Gradually add sugar and continue to whisk until light and fluffy, with soft peaks.

- Fold meringue into batter in batches until fully incorporated. Pour batter into a heated waffle iron and cook until golden brown. Repeat until ingredients are used up.

- Serve waffles warm, topped with ice cream and drizzled with strawberry coulis.

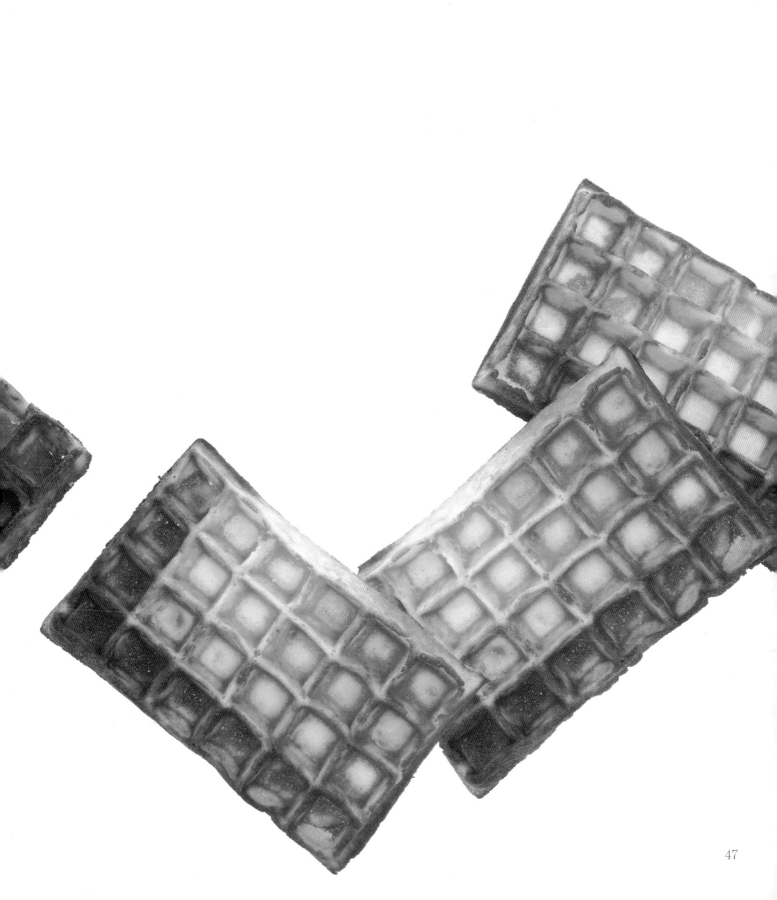

biscotti

Makes about 16

Plain (all-purpose) flour *310 g (11 oz)*	• Preheat oven to 200°C (400°F).

Plain (all-purpose) flour
310 g (11 oz)

Salt *a pinch*

Cream of tartar
5 g (¹/₆ oz)

Baking powder *2 g (¹/₇ oz)*

Butter *150 g (5¹/₃ oz)*

Sugar *250 g (9 oz)*

Vanilla essence *¹/₂ tsp*

Eggs *55 g (2 oz)*

Dried cranberries
65 g (2¹/₅ oz)

Almond nibs *65 g (2¹/₅ oz)*

Butter for greasing

Egg yolk *1, beaten*

• Preheat oven to 200°C (400°F).

• Sift flour, salt, cream of tartar and baking powder into a mixing bowl. Mix well and set aside.

• In another bowl, combine butter, sugar, vanilla essence and eggs and beat until light and fluffy. Add flour mixture, dried cranberries and almond nibs and mix on low speed to form a dough.

• Lightly grease a 20-cm (8-in) square baking pan with butter. Pack dough in firmly and evenly. Brush surface with egg yolk, then bake for 20–25 minutes or until light golden brown.

• Allow biscotti to cool, then cut into 16 bars, each about 10 x 2.5-cm (4 x 1-in) before serving.

peanut butter cookies

Makes 75–78 cookies

Plain (all-purpose) flour
180 g (6¹/₂ oz)

Salt *a pinch*

Baking soda *5 g (¹/₆ oz)*

Rolled oats *100 g (3¹/₂ oz)*

Unsalted butter *100 g (3¹/₂ oz)*

Brown sugar *200 g (7 oz)*

Smooth or chunky peanut butter
140 g (5 oz)

Egg *1*

Vanilla essence *1 tsp*

- Preheat oven to 180°C (350°F).

- Sift flour, salt and baking soda into a mixing bowl. Add oats and mix well and set aside.

- Place butter, brown sugar and peanut butter in a mixing bowl and whisk at medium speed for about 3 minutes. Add egg and vanilla essence and whisk until well blended. Add flour mixture and blend on low speed until smooth.

- Place mixture on a floured work surface and knead to form a dough. Divide dough into 2.5-cm (1-in) balls and flatten into 1-cm (¹/₂-in) thick discs.

- Arrange 2.5-cm (1-in) apart on a lined baking tray and bake for 20–25 minutes, until cookies are light golden brown. Set aside to cool before serving or storing in an airtight container.

bostock

Serves 3–4

Brioche (page 34) *1 loaf*
Almond cream (page 24) *20 g (²/₃ oz)*
Almond flakes *15 g (¹/₂ oz)*
Icing (confectioner's) sugar *for dusting*

bostock syrup

Water *125 ml (4 fl oz / ¹/₂ cup)*
Sugar *100 g (3¹/₂ oz)*
Glucose *1¹/₂ Tbsp*
Icing (confectioner's) sugar *45 g (1¹/₂ oz)*
Almond flakes *15 g (¹/₂ oz)*
Orange blossom essence *1 g (¹/₈ oz)*

- Prepare bostock syrup. Combine water, sugar and glucose in a pot and bring to the boil. Remove from heat and set aside to cool. Add icing sugar, almond flakes and orange blossom essence and stir until syrup thickens. Refrigerate until ready to use.

- Preheat oven to 180°C (350°F).

- Cut brioche into 1.5 cm (³/₄-in) thick slices. Glaze with bostock syrup, then spread a thin layer of almond cream and sprinkle almond flakes over.

- Bake for 8–10 minutes or until brioche is light golden brown. Set aside to cool. Dust with icing sugar before serving.

macarons

basic macarons with butter cream

Makes about 75 macarons

Red food colouring (optional)

Butter cream (page 31)
1 kg (2 lb 3 oz)

basic macarons

Icing (confectioner's) sugar
1 kg (2 lb 3 oz)

Ground almonds *750 g*
(1 lb 10¹/₂ oz), sifted

Egg whites *750 g*
(1 lb 10¹/₂ oz)

Sugar *370 g (13 oz)*

Powdered egg whites *70 g (2¹/₂ oz)*

- Prepare basic macarons. Combine icing sugar and almonds in a mixing bowl and mix well. Set aside.

- Combine egg whites and sugar in a mixing bowl. Place in a bain-marie and whisk constantly until sugar is completely melted. Remove from heat and whisk on medium speed for 3 minutes. Add powdered egg whites and increase to high speed. Continue to whisk until mixture is light and fluffy, with soft to medium peaks.

- Spoon half the egg white mixture into another bowl and set aside. Gradually fold icing sugar mixture into remaining egg white mixture until fully incorporated. Fold in reserved egg white mixture until batter has a slightly watery base.

- Spoon batter into a piping bag and pipe out 3-cm (¹/₄-in) circles, 1-cm (¹/₂-in) apart on lined baking trays. Leave to dry in a cool, airy place for about 30 minutes.

- Sprinkle some food colouring on macarons for some colour, if desired.

- Preheat oven to 160°C (325°F) and bake macarons for 10 minutes. Macarons should start rising after first 5 minutes. Reduce heat to 120°C (250°F) and continue baking for another 15 minutes. Remove and set aside to cool.

- Spoon butter cream into a piping bag. Pipe some cream on an overturned macaron, then sandwich with another macaron. Repeat for remaining macarons.

- Store macarons in an airtight container.

rose macarons

Basic macarons (page 52)
1 quantity
Red food colouring *1 Tbsp*

rose butter cream

Butter cream (page 31) *1 kg (2 lb 3 oz)*
Rose syrup *85 ml (2¹/₂ fl oz / ¹/₃ cup)*
Rose essence *2 tsp*

Makes about 75 macarons

- Prepare macarons. Stir in food colouring while mixing egg whites and sugar.

- Prepare rose butter cream. Combine all ingredients and mix well. Spoon butter cream into a piping bag. Pipe some cream on an overturned macaron, then sandwich with another macaron. Repeat for remaining macarons.

- Store in an airtight container.

pistachio macarons

Basic macarons (page 52)
1 quantity
Green food colouring *1 Tbsp*

pistachio butter cream

Butter cream (page 31) *500 g (1 lb 1¹/₂ oz)*
Pistachio paste *3 Tbsp*
Pistachio nuts *45 g (1¹/₂ oz), shelled and finely chopped*

Makes about 75 macarons

- Prepare macarons. Stir in food colouring while mixing egg whites and sugar.

- Prepare rose butter cream. Combine all ingredients and mix well. Spoon butter cream into a piping bag. Pipe some cream on an overturned macaron, then sandwich with another macaron. Repeat for remaining macarons.

- Store in an airtight container.

crisp chocolate chip cookies with dried cranberries and pistachios

Plain (all-purpose) flour
255 g (9 oz)

Salt *5 g ($^1/_6$ oz)*

Baking soda *5 g ($^1/_6$ oz)*

Unsalted butter
150 g (5$^1/_3$ oz), softened

Brown sugar *100 g (3$^1/_2$ oz)*

Sugar *55 g (2 oz)*

Corn syrup *3$^1/_4$ Tbsp*

Milk *2 Tbsp*

Vanilla essence *$^3/_4$ Tbsp*

Bittersweet chocolate chips
200 g (7 oz)

Pistachio nuts *100 g (3$^1/_2$ oz),
shelled and chopped*

Dried cranberries *85 g (3 oz), chopped*

Makes about 90 cookies

- Preheat oven to 180°C (350°F).

- Sift flour, salt and baking soda into a mixing bowl. Set aside.

- Place butter and sugars in another mixing bowl and whisk until light and fluffy. Add corn syrup, milk and vanilla essence and whisk until well blended.

- Add flour mixture and mix on low speed until smooth. Add chocolate chips, pistachio nuts and dried cranberries.

- Place mixture on a floured work surface and knead to form a dough. Divide dough into 2.5-cm (1-in) balls and flatten into 1-cm ($^1/_2$-in) thick discs.

- Arrange on a lined baking tray about 2.5-cm (1-in) apart and bake for 15 minutes until light golden brown. Set aside to cool before serving or storing in an airtight container.

{ cakes }

Whether prepared for a simple afternoon tea or a special occasion, cakes are always a pleasure to bake, as there is so much room for creativity. Try the Velvety Cream Cheese Pound Cake, which has a moist, delicate crumb despite its robust appearance, or the luscious Jivara Mousse, where just one mouthful is worth all the effort.

buttery orange sugee cake

Makes two 18 x 7.5-cm (7 x 3-in) cakes

sugee cake

Cake flour *160 g (5²/₃ oz)*

Baking powder *5 g (¹/₆ oz)*

Unsalted butter *400 g (14¹/₃ oz)*

Sugar *140 g (5 oz)*

Orange essence *1–2 Tbsp*

Milk *60 ml (2 fl oz / ¹/₄ cup)*

Vanilla essence *1 tsp*

Egg yolks *120 g (4 oz)*

Semolina *160 g (5²/₃ oz)*

Salt *5 g (¹/₆ oz)*

Ground almonds *45 g (1¹/₂ oz)*

Almond flakes *30 g (1 oz)*

basic meringue for sugee cake

Egg whites *240 g (8¹/₂ oz)*

Sugar *140 g (5 oz)*

- Preheat oven to 180°C (350°F).

- Prepare sugee cake. Sift flour and baking powder into a mixing bowl. Set aside.

- Place butter and sugar in another mixing bowl and beat at medium speed for 15–20 minutes or until light and fluffy and sugar is completely melted.

- Add orange essence, milk and vanilla essence and mix well. Add egg yolks, one at a time and mix well.

- Fold in flour mixture, semolina, salt and ground almonds in batches, until fully incorporated. Set aside.

- Prepare meringue. Place egg whites in a mixing bowl and whisk until foamy. Gradually add sugar and continue to whisk until light and fluffy, with soft peaks. Fold meringue gradually into batter until fully incorporated.

- Line two 18 x 7.5-cm (7 x 3-in) loaf tins. Divide batter equally into tins and level with a spatula. Sprinkle almond flakes on top and bake for 30–35 minutes, until top is golden brown and a skewer inserted into centre of cake comes out clean.

- Unmould cakes and peel off paper. Set aside to cool before serving.

strawberry shortcake

Strawberries *1 kg (2 lb 3 oz),
cleaned, hulled and sliced*

genoise sponge

Egg yolks *110 g (4 oz)*

Eggs *175 g (6¹/₅ oz)*

Sugar *170 g (6 oz)*

Light cake flour *110 g
(4 oz), sifted*

Unsalted butter *55 g (2 oz),
melted*

chantilly cream

Whipping cream *1 litre
(32 fl oz / 4 cups)*

Sugar *100 g (3¹/₂ oz)*

Mascarpone cheese *100 g
(3¹/₂ oz)*

Makes one 20-cm (8-in) cake

- Preheat oven to 180°C (350°F).

- Prepare genoise sponge. Combine egg yolks, eggs and sugar in a mixing bowl and whisk on high speed for 10 minutes. Reduce to medium speed and whisk for another 10 minutes or until fine air bubbles form.

- Lightly fold in flour, followed by melted butter, until fully incorporated.

- Pour batter into a lined 20-cm (8-in) round cake tin. Level batter with a spatula and bake for 20–25 minutes or until top of cake is firm to the touch. Remove from heat and leave aside to cool.

- Unmould cake and remove paper. Peel skin off top of cake and discard. If not using immediately, cover with plastic wrap and freeze. Genoise sponge can keep for up to 6 weeks, frozen and 3 days, refrigerated.

- Prepare chantilly cream. Combine cream, sugar and mascarpone cheese in a mixing bowl and whisk at medium speed for 3 minutes. Increase to high speed and continue to whisk until light and smooth. Set aside.

Cake assembly

- Horizontally slice genoise sponge into 2 equal layers. Place one layer on a cake board and place a 22.5-cm (9-in) cake ring over. Spoon half of chantilly cream over and around sides of sponge layer and level with an angle palette knife. Arrange some strawberries on top of cream, then place second sponge layer over. Spoon remaining cream over and around sides of cake and level again. Refrigerate cake until slightly firm.

- Gently ease cake ring from cake and remove. Coat side of cake with ground almonds, if desired. Decorate cake as desired and serve chilled.

frasier

Makes one 40 x 25-cm (16 x 10-in) cake

almond genoise sponge

Cake flour *70 g* *(2¹/₂ oz)*

Baking powder *5 g (¹/₆ oz)*

Almond paste *370 ml (13 oz)*

Eggs *400 g (14¹/₃ oz)*

Unsalted butter *115 g (4¹/₅ oz), melted*

pistachio butter cream

Whipping cream *250 ml (8 fl oz / 1 cup)*

Butter cream (page 31) *500 g (1 lb 1¹/₂ oz)*

Pistachio paste *2 Tbsp*

Crème patisserie (page 23) *250 g (9 oz)*

kirsch strawberries

Kirsch liqueur (Kirschwasser) *2 Tbsp*

Sugar *30 g (1 oz)*

Strawberries *1 kg (2 lb 3 oz), cleaned and hulled*

italian meringue

Sugar *100 g (4¹/₂ oz)*

Water *2 Tbsp*

Egg whites *55 g (2 oz)*

- Preheat oven to 180°C (350°F).

- Prepare almond genoise sponge. Sift flour and baking powder into a mixing bowl and set aside.

- Beat almond paste in a mixing bowl at medium speed, then add half the eggs, one at a time, and mix well. Add remaining eggs, one at a time, and whisk at medium speed until light and fluffy. Increase to high speed and whisk for another 2 minutes. Mixture should have doubled in volume and be pale yellow.

- Place melted butter in another mixing bowl. Fold in flour mixture until fully incorporated, then repeat to fold in egg mixture.

- Pour batter into a lined 40 x 25 x 3-cm (16 x 10 x 1-in) baking tray. Level batter with a spatula and bake for 15–20 minutes or until top is firm to the touch. Remove from heat and unmould cake. Peel off paper and set aside to cool.

- Cover cooled genoise sponge with plastic wrap and freeze. Genoise sponge can keep for up to 6 weeks, frozen and 3 days, refrigerated.

- Prepare butter cream. Place whipping cream in a mixing bowl and whisk until light and fluffy. Refrigerate to chill. Combine butter cream and pistachio paste in a mixing bowl and whisk for 5 minutes or until light and fluffy. Fold crème patisserie into chilled whipped cream, then fold into butter cream mixture evenly. Set aside.

- Prepare strawberries. Combine kirsch and sugar in a large bowl and mix until most of sugar is dissolved. Place strawberries in to steep for 30 minutes. Drain and set aside.

Cake assembly

- Horizontally slice genoise sponge into 2 equal layers. Pour half of butter cream over sponge layer and level with an angle palette knife.

- Arrange strawberries on top of cream layer, then pour remaining cream over strawberries and level. Sandwich with second sponge layer, then refrigerate until butter cream is slightly firm.

- Meanwhile, prepare meringue. Combine sugar and water in a saucepan and bring to 117°C (243°F). Pour into egg whites and beat until meringue is shiny and smooth, with stiff peaks. Using an angle palette knife, spread meringue over genoise sponge. Refrigerator for 1–2 hours.

- Using a blowtorch, caramelise surface of meringue until light golden brown. Slice and serve with fresh fruit, if desired.

chocolate brownie

Makes one 28-cm (11-in) square cake

Plain (all-purpose) flour *325 g (11¹/₂ oz)*

Baking powder *5 g (¹/₆ oz)*

Cocoa powder *150 g (5¹/₃ oz), sifted*

Cream cheese *225 g (8 oz)*

Sugar *860 g (1⁴/₅ lb)*

Vanilla essence *¹/₂ tsp*

Salt *10 g (¹/₃ oz)*

Unsalted butter *450 g (16 oz)*

Eggs *400 g (14¹/₃ oz)*

Walnuts *300 g (10¹/₂ oz), chopped*

Butter *for greasing*

- Preheat oven to 180°C (350°F).

- Sift flour, baking powder and cocoa powder into a mixing bowl and set aside.

- Place cream cheese, sugar, vanilla essence, salt and butter in another mixing bowl and whisk until well blended.

- Fold eggs into cream cheese mixture, then gradually fold in flour, mixture. Add walnuts and mix well.

- Lightly grease a 28-cm (11-in) square baking tin with butter. Level batter into tin and bake for 20 minutes.

- Unmould brownie and leave aside to cool. Slice before serving.

velvety cream cheese pound cake

Makes three 18 x 7.5-cm (7 x 3-in) cakes

pound cake

Cake flour *400 g (14¹/₃ oz)*

Salt *6 g (¹/₅ oz)*

Cream cheese *20 g (²/₃ oz)*

Unsalted butter *250 g (9 oz)*

Sugar *160 g (5²/₃ oz)*

Egg yolks *170 g (6 oz)*

Vanilla essence *1 Tbsp*

Parmesan cheese *20 g (²/₃ oz)*

basic meringue for pound cake

Egg whites *250 g (9 oz)*

Sugar *250 g (9 oz)*

cream cheese glaze

Cream cheese *140 g (5 oz)*

Unsalted butter *10 g (¹/₃ oz)*

Vanilla essence *¹/₂ tsp*

Lemon *1, small, grated for zest and squeezed for 1 tsp juice*

Icing (confectioner's) sugar *45 g (1¹/₂ oz)*

parmesan wafers (optional)

Parmesan cheese *30 g (1 oz)*

- Preheat oven to 180°C (350°F). Line 3 loaf tins, each 18 x 7.5-cm (7 x 3-in) and set aside.

- Prepare pound cakes. Sift flour and salt and sift into a mixing bowl. Set aside.

- Beat cream cheese, butter and sugar until light and fluffy. Gradually add egg yolks, vanilla essence and Parmesan cheese and stir until well blended. Fold in flour mixture and set aside.

- Prepare meringue. Place egg whites in a mixing bowl and whisk until foamy. Gradually add sugar and continue to whisk until light and fluffy, with medium peaks.

- Fold meringue into batter and pour into prepared loaf tins. Bake for 25–30 minutes until a skewer inserted into the centre of cake comes out clean. Remove cakes from tins and peel off paper. Set aside to cool.

- Prepare cream cheese glaze. Beat cream cheese, butter and vanilla essence until light and fluffy. Add lemon zest and juice and icing sugar and mix well. Set aside.

- Prepare Parmesan wafers, if desired. Sprinkle a thin layer of Parmesan cheese on a lightly greased baking tray and bake in a preheated oven at 180°C (350°F) until golden brown. Set aside to cool before cutting into desired shapes.

- Use a palette knife to spread cream cheese glaze over cake. Decorate with Parmesan cheese wafers, or as desired, and serve.

chocolate crunch cake

Makes three 18 x 7.5-cm (7 x 3-in) cakes

cake

Sugar *100 g (3¹/₂ oz)*

Water *200 ml (7 fl oz / ⁴/₅ cups)*

Freshly squeezed orange juice
100 ml (3¹/₂ fl oz / ²/₅ cup)

Raisins *200 g (7 oz)*

Cake flour *380 g (13¹/₂ oz)*

Cocoa powder *100 g (3¹/₂ oz)*

Baking powder *8 g (¹/₃ oz)*

Unsalted butter *500 g (1 lb 1¹/₂ oz)*

Sugar *250 g (9 oz)*

Egg yolks *200 g (7 oz)*

Valrhona Tropilia 53% chocolate
100 g (3¹/₂ oz), roughly chopped

basic meringue for cake

Egg whites *300 g (10¹/₂ oz)*

Sugar *250 g (9 oz)*

bitter chocolate frosting

Valrhona Cacao Pâte Extra 100%
45 g (1¹/₂ oz)

Unsalted butter *70 g (2¹/₂ oz)*

Icing (confectioner's) sugar
85 g (3 oz)

Egg *30 g (1 oz)*

Lemon juice *¹/₂ tsp*

Vanilla essence *1 Tbsp*

- Preheat oven to 180°C (350°F). Line 3 loaf tins, each 18 x 7.5-cm (7 x 3-in) and set aside.

- Prepare cake. Combine sugar and water and bring to the boil, stirring constantly until sugar is completely dissolved. Remove from heat and stir in orange juice. Set aside to cool, then add raisins and refrigerate.

- Sift flour, cocoa powder and baking powder into a mixing bowl and set aside.

- Place butter, sugar and egg yolks in a mixing bowl and whisk until light and fluffy. Add chocolate and mix well, then fold in flour mixture.

- Prepare meringue. Place egg whites in a mixing bowl and whisk until foamy. Gradually add sugar and continue to whisk until light and fluffy, with medium peaks.

- Drain raisins and add to batter, then fold in meringue. Pour batter into prepared loaf tins and bake for 30–35 minutes until a skewer inserted into the centre of cake comes out clean. Remove from heat. Remove cakes from tins and peel off paper. Set aside to cool.

- Prepare chocolate frosting. Melt chocolate in a bain-marie to 60°C (140°F). Transfer chocolate to a mixing bowl and add butter. Mix on low speed until well blended. Gradually add icing sugar and mix well, then add egg, lemon juice and vanilla essence and mix well again.

- Using a palette knife, spread chocolate frosting over top of each cake. Decorate as desired before serving.

coco ananas

Makes one 15-cm (6-in) round cake

coconut sponge cake

Almond powder *55 g (2 oz)*

Desiccated coconut *55 g (2 oz)*

Sugar *125 g (4¹/₂ oz)*

Icing (confectioner's) sugar *115 g (4¹/₅ oz)*

Whipping cream *2¹/₂ Tbsp*

Plain (all-purpose) flour *85 g (3 oz), sifted*

basic meringue for coconut sponge cake

Egg whites *230 g (8 oz)*

Sugar *125 g (4¹/₂ oz)*

coconut mousse

Whipping cream *150 ml (5¹/₃ fl oz / ³/₅ cup)*

Coconut purée *250 ml (8 fl oz / 1 cup)*

Gelatine sheets *5 g (¹/₆ oz)*

italian meringue for coconut mousse

Water *125 ml (4 fl oz / ¹/₂ cup)*

Sugar *110 g (4 oz)*

Egg whites *75 g (2³/₅ oz)*

- Preheat oven to 200°C (400°F).

- Prepare sponge cake. Combine almond powder, coconut, sugar and icing sugar in a mixing bowl. Add whipping cream and mix until well blended. Set aside.

- Prepare basic meringue. Place egg whites in a mixing bowl and whisk until foamy. Gradually add sugar and continue to whisk until light and fluffy, with soft peaks. Fold half of meringue into sponge mixture, then fold in flour before folding in remaining meringue.

- Pour batter into a 25 x 30-cm (10 x 12-in) baking tray and bake for 10–15 minutes. Insert a skewer into the centre of cake. The skewer should come out clean. Remove from heat and set aside to cool.

- Prepare mousse. Pour whipping cream into a mixing bowl and whip until soft to medium peaks form. Refrigerate to chill.

- Heat half of coconut purée in a bain-marie to 50°C (122°F). Add softened gelatine and stir until dissolved. Remove from heat and set aside.

- Prepare Italian meringue. Combine water and sugar in a saucepan and bring to 117°C (243°F) over low heat, stirring until sugar is completely dissolved. Gradually add to egg whites and beat until stiff peaks form and meringue is shiny and smooth.

- Fold meringue into coconut-gelatine mixture, then fold in remaining coconut purée. Add chilled whipped cream and fold in until fully incorporated.

- Using a 15-cm (6-in) cake ring, cut out 2 sponge circles from cooled cake. Place one sponge circle on a cake tray and place a slightly wider cake ring over cake. Spoon half of coconut mousse over top and around sides of cake. Smoothen with a spatula. Place second sponge layer over mousse and pour remaining mousse over top and around sides of cake. Repeat to smoothen with a spatula.

- Gently ease cake ring from cake. Decorate cake with cream, desiccated coconut and fresh fruit as desired before serving.

jivara mousse

Makes one 20-cm (8-in) square cake

sacher sponge

Cocoa powder 20 g (2/3 oz)

Plain (all-purpose) flour
45 g (1 1/2 oz)

Almond paste 150 ml
(5 1/3 fl oz / 3/5 cup)

Sugar 30 g (1 oz)

Egg 55 g (2 oz)

Egg yolks 70 g (2 1/2 oz)

Dark chocolate 45 g
(1 1/2 oz), finely chopped

Butter 45 g (1 1/2 oz)

basic meringue for sacher sponge

Egg whites 100 g (3 1/2 oz)

Sugar 60 g (2 oz)

jivara mousse

Valrhona Jivara chocolate (70%)
280 g (10 oz)

Whipping cream 500 ml
(16 fl oz / 2 cups)

jivara crunch

Valrhona Jivara chocolate (70%)
55 g (2 oz)

Pailleté feuilletine (crushed wafer
flakes) 100 g (3 1/2 oz)

Butter 25 g (4/5 oz)

Hazelnut praline 175 g (6 1/5 oz)

- Preheat oven to 180°C (350°F).

- Prepare Sacher sponge. Sift cocoa powder and flour into a mixing bowl and set aside.

- Place almond paste and sugar into another mixing bowl and beat at medium speed until well-mixed, then increase to high speed and beat until sugar is completely melted. Add egg and mix well. Add egg yolks, one at a time, and whisk at medium speed for 5 minutes or until light and fluffy. Set aside.

- Place chocolate and butter in a pot and stir over low heat until melted. Do not let chocolate burn. Remove from heat and set aside.

- Prepare basic meringue. Place egg whites in a mixing bowl and whisk until foamy. Gradually add sugar and continue to whisk until light and fluffy, with medium peaks.

- Fold chocolate mixture into almond mixture, then fold in meringue until fully incorporated.

- Pour batter into a lined 22-cm (9-in) square baking tin. Level batter with a spatula and bake for 15–20 minutes until sponge is firm to the touch. Remove from heat. Unmould sponge and set aside to cool.

- Prepare Jivara mousse. Melt chocolate in a bain-marie to 45°C (113°F). Whisk cream until light and fluffy, then fold into chocolate until fully incorporated. Set aside.

- Prepare Jivara crunch. Melt chocolate in a bain-marie. Transfer to a mixing bowl and add feuilletine. Mix to coat evenly and set aside. Melt butter in a saucepan until lightly browned and pour over chocolate mixture. Add hazelnut praline and mix well. Set aside.

Cake assembly

- Assemble cake. Line a 20-cm (8-in) square baking tin. Scoop Jivara crunch mixture into tin and level with a spatula to create the base.

- Cut sponge slightly smaller than baking tin and place over base. Spoon Jivara mousse over sponge. Create a pattern with mousse as desired, then refrigerate until mousse is slightly firm.

- Carefully remove cake from baking tin and peel off paper. Decorate as desired and serve chilled.

zesty lemon pound cake

Cake flour *400 g (14¹/₃ oz)*

Baking soda *5 g (¹/₆ oz)*

Salt *15 g (¹/₂ oz)*

Lemons *1, large, grated for zest and squeezed for 60 ml (2 fl oz / ¹/₄ cup) juice*

Frozen semi-candied lemons *60 g (2 oz)*

Cream cheese *180 g (6³/₅ oz)*

Unsalted butter *200 g (7 oz)*

Sugar *240 g (8¹/₂ oz)*

Vanilla essence *2 Tbsp*

Egg yolks *110 g (4 oz)*

Cream cheese glaze *(page 67) 1 quantity*

basic meringue

Egg whites *160 g (5²/₃ oz)*

Sugar *160 g (5²/₃ oz)*

- Preheat oven to 180°C (350°F). Line 3 loaf tins, each 18 x 7.5-cm (7 x 3-in) and set aside.

- Sift flour, baking soda and salt into a mixing bowl and set aside.

- Combine lemon zest, lemon juice and candied lemons in another mixing bowl and mix well. Set aside.

- Place cream cheese, butter, sugar and vanilla essence in a mixing bowl and beat at medium speed for 15–20 minutes until light and fluffy. Gradually add egg yolks and lemon mixture until well incorporated. Fold in flour mixture and set aside.

- Prepare meringue. Place egg whites in a mixing bowl and whisk until foamy. Gradually add sugar and continue to whisk until light and fluffy, with soft peaks. Fold meringue into batter until fully incorporated.

- Pour batter into prepared loaf tins and bake for 30–35 minutes until a skewer inserted into the centre of cake comes out clean. Remove from heat and set aside to cool.

- Spread cream cheese glaze over cakes. Decorate as desired before serving.

amer mousse with flourless chocolate sponge

Makes one 15-cm (6-in) cake

flourless chocolate sponge

Egg yolks *120 g (4 oz)*

Sugar *100 g (3¹/₂ oz)*

Cocoa powder *55 g (2 oz), sifted*

basic meringue for flourless chocolate sponge

Egg whites *150 g (5¹/₃ oz)*

Sugar *100 g (3¹/₂ oz)*

chocolate mousse

Eggs *280 g (10 oz)*

Sugar *85 g (3 oz)*

Gelatine sheets *5 g (¹/₆ oz), soaked in ice water until softened and drained*

Valrhona Pur Caraibe 66% chocolate *100 g (3¹/₂ oz)*

Valrhona Tropilia 53% chocolate *110 g (4 oz)*

Butter *85 g (3 oz)*

Cocoa powder *25 g (⁴/₅ oz), sifted*

Whipping cream *435 ml (14 fl oz / 1³/₄ cups)*

- Preheat oven to 200°C (400°F).

- Prepare flourless chocolate sponge. Place egg yolks and sugar in a mixing bowl and beat at high speed until light and fluffy. Set aside.

- Prepare basic meringue. Place egg whites in a mixing bowl and whisk until foamy. Gradually add sugar and continue to whisk until light and fluffy, with soft peaks. Fold egg yolk mixture into meringue, then fold in cocoa powder until fully incorporated.

- Pour batter into a lined 32 x 16-cm (13 x 6.5-in) baking tin and bake for 8–10 minutes. Remove from oven and unmould cake. Peel off paper and set aside to cool. Cut cake into two 16-cm (6.5-in) square cakes and set aside.

- Prepare chocolate mousse. Crack eggs into a mixing bowl and whisk. Bring sugar to 120°C (250°F) and add to eggs.

- Melt gelatine in a bain-marie and set aside.

- Melt both types of chocolate and butter in a bain-marie until mixture heats to 55°C (131°F). Add cocoa powder and gelatine and whisk until smooth and well blended. Set aside.

- Whisk whipping cream until light and fluffy. Fold half of whipped cream into chocolate mixture until fully incorporated. Add to egg mixture, then fold in remaining whipped cream.

- Place a chocolate sponge on a cake board. Using a palette knife, spread mousse over evenly, then sandwich with other sponge cake. Decorate as desired and refrigerate until well-chilled before serving.

coeur noir (black heart)

Makes two 18-cm (7-in) cakes

Sacher sponge (page 72) *1 quantity*

Griotte cherries *100 g (3¹/₂ oz)*

hazelnut dacquoise

Sugar *15 g (¹/₂ oz)*

Liquid egg whites *125 ml (4 fl oz / ¹/₂ cup)*

Icing (confectioner's) sugar *100 g (3¹/₂ oz)*

Blanched hazelnuts *140 g (5 oz), finely ground*

Hazelnuts *70 g (2¹/₂ oz), chopped*

chocolate mousse

Liquid egg yolks *3¹/₂ Tbsp*

Sugar *55 g (2 oz)*

Valrhona Manjari (64%) chocolate *280 g (10 oz)*

Milk *90 ml (3 fl oz / ³/₈ cup)*

Whipping cream *90 ml (3 fl oz / ³/₈ cup)*

chocolate glaze

Whipping cream *200 ml (24 fl oz / 3 cups)*

Sugar *320 g (11¹/₃ oz)*

Water *180 ml (6 fl oz / ³/₄ cup)*

Glucose *250 ml (8 fl oz / 1 cup)*

Gelatine powder *20 g (²/₃ oz), sifted*

Cocoa powder *110 g (4 oz), sifted*

- Prepare Sacher sponge and level batter into a lined 18-cm (7-in) heart-shaped baking tin. Bake in a preheated oven at 180°C (350°F) for 15–20 minutes until sponge is firm to the touch. Remove from heat. Unmould cake and set aside to cool. Cover with plastic wrap and refrigerate until ready to use.

- Prepare hazelnut dacquoise. Place sugar and egg whites in a mixing bowl and whisk to combine. Fold in icing sugar and blanched hazelnuts until fully incorporated, then add chopped hazelnuts and mix well. Pour into two heart-shaped baking tins the same size used for sponge and level evenly with a spatula. Bake in a preheated oven at 200°C (400°F) for 15 minutes or until golden brown. Remove from heat and set aside to cool.

- Prepare mousse. Place egg yolks in a mixing bowl and set aside. Heat sugar in a saucepan to 120°C (250°F), then gradually pour into egg yolks and stir to mix well. Set aside.

- Place chocolate in another mixing bowl and set aside. Bring milk to the boil and gradually pour over chocolate while stirring. Stir until chocolate is 55°C (131°F) and completely melted. Fold in whipping cream, then fold mixture into egg yolk mixture. Refrigerate until ready to use.

- Prepare two heart-shaped cake rings slightly larger than sponge cakes. Set aside.

- Cut cake horizontally into two layers and set aside. Fit a cake ring over each dacquoise and place on a baking tray. Spoon chocolate mousse into a piping bag and pipe a layer over dacquoise. Arrange cherries on top of mousse, then sandwich with a sponge cake. Pipe more mousse over sponge and cover with plastic wrap. Refrigerator for 1–2 hours until mousse is firm.

- Meanwhile, prepare chocolate glaze. Combine whipping cream, sugar and 90 ml (3 fl oz / ³/₈ cup) water in a pot and bring to the boil. Add glucose and stir to mix well. Remove from heat, then stir in gelatine and cocoa powders and remaining water. Beat on medium speed until smooth and shiny. Strain to remove any lumps.

- Unmould cakes from rings and place on a wire rack over the sink. Pour glaze over cakes until completely coated. Leave so excess glaze can drip off. Place cakes on desired cake boards and return to the refrigerator to chill and set.

- Decorate cakes as desired and serve chilled.

{ jellies and puddings }

With their attractive colours, jellies and puddings have always been a hit with children. The jellies and puddings featured here are "grown-up" versions of simple but elegant desserts.

kirsch jelly

Makes 8–10 small glasses

Sugar *100 g (3¹/₂ oz)*

Agar agar powder *1 g (¹/₈ oz)*

Water *500 ml (16 fl oz / 2 cups)*

Gelatine sheets *10 g (¹/₃ oz), soaked in ice water to soften and drained*

Lemon juice *1 Tbsp*

Kirsch liqueur (Kirschwasser) *2¹/₂ Tbsp*

Fresh fruit of choice

- Start preparations 1 day ahead, as jelly takes time to set.

- Place sugar, agar agar powder and water in a pot. Bring to the boil over low heat, stirring until sugar and agar agar powder are completely dissolved. Remove from heat and stir in softened gelatine until completely melted. Stir in lemon juice and kirsch and set aside to cool.

- Place some fruit into 8–10 small glasses. Pour in enough jelly to just cover fruit. Refrigerate for 1–2 hours until slightly firm.

- Reheat remaining jelly mixture a little if it has set. Spoon into glasses over set jelly, leaving enough space for garnish, if desired. Return to the refrigerator to set.

- Garnish as desired and serve chilled.

passion fruit panna cotta

Makes 3–4 small glasses

vanilla panna cotta

Single (light) cream *350 ml*
(12 1/3 fl oz / 1 2/5 cups)

Sugar *45 g (1 1/2 oz)*

Vanilla bean *1/2, scraped for seeds*
and reserve pod, or use 1 tsp
vanilla essence

Water *1 Tbsp*

Gelatine sheets *2 g (1/7 oz), soaked*
in ice water to soften and drained

passion fruit coulis

Pectin *1 tsp*

Passion fruit purée *60 ml*
(2 1/2 fl oz / 1/3 cup)

Sugar *45 g (1 1/2 oz)*

Gelatine sheet *1/2 sheet, soaked in*
ice water to soften and drained

garnish (optional)

Fresh fruit of choice

Chopped nuts

- Prepare vanilla panna cotta. Place cream, sugar, vanilla pod and seeds or vanilla essence and water in a pot. Bring to a gentle simmer over medium heat, stirring until sugar is completely dissolved. Stir in softened gelatine until completely melted. Strain mixture and set aside to cool before pouring into 3–4 small glasses. Refrigerate for about 3 hours, or until set.

- Prepare passion fruit coulis. Place pectin, passion fruit, purée and sugar in a pot over low heat. Bring to the boil, stirring until sugar is completely dissolved. Stir in gelatine until completely melted. Remove from heat and set aside to cool. Refrigerate until chilled.

- Spoon passion fruit coulis over vanilla panna cotta. Garnish with fresh fruit and nuts, if desired. Serve chilled.

coffee caramel panna cotta

Vanilla panna cotta (page 85)
3–4 glasses

caramel coffee cream

Single (light) cream *500 ml
(16 fl oz / 2 cups)*

Sugar *750 g (1 lb 10¹/₂ oz)*

Instant coffee granules
70 g (2¹/₂ oz)

Hot water *250 ml
(8 fl oz / 1 cup)*

Gelatine sheet, *2 g (¹/₇ oz), soaked
in ice water to soften and drained*

garnish (optional)

Gold flakes

Biscotti (page 48) *3–4 slices*

Makes 3–4 small glasses

- Prepare caramel coffee cream. Warm cream over low heat and set aside. Caramelise 500 g (1 lb 1¹/₂ oz) sugar over low heat, stirring constantly until sugar is completely melted and dark golden brown in colour. Stir in cream and remove from heat. Set aside.

- Dissolve coffee granules in hot water. Set aside.

- Combine cream mixture, coffee and softened gelatine in a pot over low heat and stir until gelatine is completely dissolved and mixture is thick. Remove from heat and set aside to cool before refrigerating to chill.

- Drizzle coffee caramel cream over vanilla panna cotta. Garnish with gold flakes, if desired. Serve chilled, with biscotti on the side.

ginger milk pudding

Makes 3 small glasses

Ginger juice *2 Tbsp*

Milk *180 ml (6 fl oz / ³/₄ cups)*

Single (light) cream *2¹/₄ Tbsp*

Sugar *20 g (²/₃ oz)*

- Prepare 3 serving glasses and spoon 1 Tbsp ginger juice into each glass. Set aside.

- Combine milk and cream in a pot and bring to the boil. Remove from heat and add sugar, stirring constantly until sugar is completely dissolved and mixture cools to 85°C (185°F).

- Pour milk mixture into prepared glasses and leave aside to set. Garnish as desired. Serve warm.

raspberry panna cotta

Vanilla panna cotta (page 85)
3–4 glasses

raspberry sauce

Raspberry purée 85 ml
(2¹/₂ fl oz / ¹/₃ cups)

Sugar 20 g (²/₃ oz)

Gelatine sheet 1 g (¹/₈ oz), soaked in
ice water to soften and drained

garnish (optional)

Fresh fruit of choice

Mint leaves

Makes 3–4 small glasses

- Prepare raspberry sauce. Place water, raspberry purée and sugar in a pot. Bring to the boil over low heat, stirring until sugar is completely dissolved. Stir in softened gelatine until completely melted. Remove from heat and set aside to cool before placing in the refrigerator to chill.

- Spoon raspberry sauce over vanilla panna cotta. Garnish with fresh fruit and mint leaves, if desired. Serve chilled.

bailey's soufflé

Makes 1 small soufflé

Unsalted butter *for greasing ramekin*

Sugar *for coating ramekin*

Egg *30 g (1 oz),*
yolk and white separated

Sugar *1 Tbsp*

Bailey's liqueur *1 Tbsp*

- Preheat oven to 180°C (350°F).

- Prepare an 8-cm (3-in) wide and 4.5-cm (2-in) deep ramekin. Brush the inside of ramekin upwards with butter. Spoon some sugar into ramekin, then tilt ramekin around to coat sides with sugar. Overturn ramekin and discard excess sugar.

- Place egg white in a small mixing bowl and whisk until foamy. Add sugar and whisk until light and fluffy, with soft peaks.

- Place egg yolk in another mixing bowl and gradually add half of egg white mixture while stirring constantly with a spatula. Stir until well combined, then whisk in remaining egg white mixture and liqueur.

- Pour batter into ramekin until the brim and bake for 8–10 minutes until soufflé is well-risen. Serve immediately.

chocolate soufflé

Unsalted butter *for greasing ramekin*
Sugar *for coating ramekin*
Egg whites *55 g (2 oz)*
Lemon juice *1 tsp*
Sugar *1 tsp*
Chocolate *70 g (2¹/₂ oz), chopped*
Chopped nuts *(optional)*

Makes 1 small soufflé

- Preheat oven to 180°C (350°F).

- Prepare an 8-cm (3-in) wide and 4.5-cm (2-in) deep ramekin. Brush the inside of ramekin upwards with butter. Spoon some sugar into ramekin, then tilt ramekin around to coat sides with sugar. Overturn ramekin and discard excess sugar.

- Place egg whites in a small mixing bowl and whisk until foamy. Add lemon juice and sugar and whisk until light and fluffy, with soft peaks.

- Melt chocolate in a bain-marie and transfer to a mixing bowl. Gradually fold egg white mixture into melted chocolate.

- Pour batter into ramekin until the brim and bake for 8–10 minutes until soufflé is well-risen. Garnish as desired and serve immediately.

{ tarts }

There is nothing more pleasurable than tucking into a slice of homemade tart for dessert or tea. Every mouthful is a sensory experience. Buttery tart pastry combines with delicate pastry cream and sweet, fresh fruit to produce an explosion of flavours. Go ahead and experiment with other fruit and fillings of choice.

sour cherry tart

Makes one 19-cm (7½-in) tart

Sablé dough (page 31) *200 g (7 oz)*

Almond cream (page 24) *470 g (1 lb 1³/₅ oz)*

Sour cherries *360 g (12²/₃ oz), pitted*

Crumble dough (page 27) *400 g (14¹/₃ oz)*

Icing (confectioner's) sugar *for dusting*

- Preheat oven at 180°C (350°F).

- On a floured work surface, roll out sablé dough into a 0.2-cm (¹/₁₀-in) thick sheet, large enough to line the base and sides of a 19 x 2-cm (7½ x 1-in) tart pan.

- Line pan and trim edges to neaten. Spoon in almond cream to fill half of pan. Spread cream out evenly with an angle palette knife.

- Arrange sour cherries on top of cream and sprinkle crumble dough over. Bake for 20–30 minutes or until golden brown. Remove from heat and set aside to cool slightly.

- Dust with icing sugar and serve warm.

strawberry tart

Makes one 19-cm (7½-in) tart

Sablé dough (page 31) *200 g (7 oz)*

Almond cream (page 24) *470 g (1 lb 1³/₅ oz)*

Strawberries *450 g (16 oz), cleaned, hulled and sliced*

Blueberries and raspberries *(optional)*

Apricot glaze *for glazing*

Icing (confectioner's) sugar *for dusting*

- Preheat oven to 180°C (350°F).

- On a floured work surface, roll out sablé dough into a 0.2-cm (¹/₁₀-in) thick sheet, large enough to line the base and sides of a 19 x 2-cm (7½ x 1-in) tart pan.

- Line pan and trim edges to neaten. Spoon in almond cream to fill half of pan. Spread cream out evenly with an angle palette knife.

- Bake for 20–30 minutes or until golden brown. Remove from heat and set aside to cool slightly.

- Arrange strawberries and other berries, if desired, on tart and brush with apricot glaze. Dust with icing sugar and serve warm.

apple tart

Makes one 19-cm (7½-in) tart

Sablé dough (page 31) *200 g (7 oz)*

Almond cream (page 24) *470 g (1 lb 1⅗ oz)*

Green apples *5, cored and thinly sliced*

Apricot glaze *for glazing*

- Preheat oven to 180°C (350°F).

- On a floured work surface, roll out sablé dough into a 0.2-cm (¹/₁₀-in) thick sheet, large enough to line the base and sides of a 19 x 2-cm (7½ x 1-in) tart pan.

- Line pan and trim edges to neaten. Spoon in almond cream to fill half of pan. Spread cream out evenly with an angle palette knife.

- Arrange apple slices on top of cream. Bake for 20–30 minutes or until golden brown. Remove from heat and set aside to cool slightly.

- Brush top of tart with apricot glaze and serve warm.

pear tart

Makes one 19-cm (7¹/₂-in) tart

Sablé dough (page 31) *200 g (7 oz)*

Almond cream (page 24) *470 g (1 lb 1³/₅ oz)*

Pears *5, large, cored and finely sliced*

Apricot glaze *for glazing*

- Preheat oven to 180°C (350°F).

- On a floured work surface, roll out sablé dough into a 0.2-cm (¹/₁₀-in) thick sheet, large enough to line the base and sides of a 19 x 2-cm (7¹/₂ x 1-in) tart pan.

- Line pan and trim edges to neaten. Spoon in almond cream to fill half of pan. Spread cream out evenly with an angle palette knife.

- Arrange pear slices on top of cream. Bake for 20–30 minutes or until golden brown. Remove from heat and set aside to cool slightly.

- Brush top of tart with apricot glaze. Garnish as desired and serve warm.

lemon tart

Sablé dough (page 31) *200 g (7 oz)*

Lemon cream (page 27) *600 g (1 lb 5 oz)*

italian meringue

Water *3¹/₂ Tbsp*

Sugar *150 g (5¹/₃ oz)*

Egg whites *70 g (2¹/₂ oz)*

Makes one 19-cm (7¹/₂-in) tart

- Preheat oven at 180°C (350°F).

- On a floured work surface, roll out sablé dough into a 0.2-cm (¹/₁₀-in) thick sheet, large enough to line the base and sides of a 19 x 2-cm (7¹/₂ x 1-in) tart pan.

- Line pan and trim edges to neaten. Fill with baking weights and bake for 20–30 minutes or until golden brown. Remove weights and set tart shell aside to cool.

- Spoon lemon cream into tart shell until just under the brim and spread evenly with an angle palette knife.

- Prepare Italian meringue. Combine water and sugar in a saucepan and bring to 117°C (243°F) over low heat, stirring until sugar is completely dissolved. Pour syrup gradually into egg whites and beat until stiff peaks form and meringue is shiny and smooth.

- Spoon meringue into a piping bag and pipe a bold zigzag pattern across surface of lemon cream. Lightly caramelise meringue using a blow torch.

- Garnish as desired and serve.

peach tart

Sablé dough (page 31) *200 g (7 oz)*

Almond cream (page 24) *470 g (1 lb 1⅗ oz)*

Fresh peaches *25, pitted and halved*

Sugar (optional) *1–2 Tbsp*

Apricot glaze *for glazing*

- Preheat oven to 180°C (350°F).

- On a floured work surface, roll out sablé dough into a 0.2-cm (1/10-in) thick sheet, large enough to line the base and sides of a 19 x 2-cm (7½ x 1-in) tart pan.

- Line pan and trim edges to neaten. Spoon in almond cream to fill half of pan. Spread cream out evenly with an angle palette knife.

- Arrange peach halves in a fan shape on top of cream. Sprinkle sugar over to reduce tartness of peaches, if desired.

- Bake for 20–30 minutes or until golden brown. Remove from heat and set aside to cool slightly.

- Brush top of tart with apricot glaze and serve warm.

{ ices }

Whether served as an accompaniment to
a slice of fruit tart, as a topping over a slice of warm
chocolate cake, or on its own as a cooling treat
on a hot summer's day, ice creams and sorbets
never fail to refresh and whet an appetite for dessert.
Lose yourself in the luscious, velvety depths of
these ice creams and tickle your taste buds with the
refreshing, tangy sorbet concoctions.
Most of all, take pleasure and pride in creating
your own homemade ices.

mango passion sorbet

Makes about 650 g (1²/₅ lb)

Mango purée *175 ml (5⁴/₅ fl oz / ³/₅ cups)*

Passion fruit purée *75 ml (2¹/₄ fl oz / ²/₅ cup)*

Milk *75 ml (2¹/₄ fl oz / ²/₅ cup)*

Water *175 ml (5⁴/₅ fl oz / ³/₅ cups)*

Sugar *140 g (5 oz)*

Glucose powder *1 Tbsp*

- Combine mango purée, passion fruit purée, milk and water in a mixing bowl and mix well.

- Combine sugar and glucose in another mixing bowl and mix well. Gradually add mango and passion fruit mixture and whisk to combine. Cover loosely with plastic wrap and refrigerate for 2–3 hours.

- Transfer chilled mixture to an ice cream maker and churn according to the manufacturer's instructions. Store in the freezer.

chocolate sorbet

Makes about 540 g (1¹/₅ lb)

Water *350 ml (11⁴/₅ fl oz / 1²/₅ cups)*

Valrhona Pur Caraibe 66% chocolate *100 g (3¹/₂ oz), finely chopped*

Inverted sugar syrup (trimoline) *2 Tbsp*

Sugar *45 g (1¹/₂ oz)*

Glucose powder *1 Tbsp*

- Bring water to the boil in a saucepan over low heat. Gradually add chocolate and sugar syrup and mix to combine. Remove from heat and set aside.

- Combine sugar and glucose in a mixing bowl and mix well. Gradually add chocolate mixture and whisk to combine. Cover loosely with plastic wrap and refrigerate for 2–3 hours.

- Transfer chilled mixture to an ice cream maker and churn according to the manufacturer's instructions. Store in the freezer.

From left: Mango Passion Sorbet, Chocolate Sorbet

lime sorbet

Makes about 500 g (1 lb 1½ oz)

Limes *2*

Lime purée *150 ml*
(5⅓ fl oz / ⅗ cup)

Water *200 ml (7 fl oz / ⅘ cups)*

Sugar *110 g (4 oz)*

Glucose powder *30 g (1 oz)*

- Extract juice from limes into a mixing bowl. Add lime purée and water and mix well. Set aside.

- Combine sugar and glucose in a mixing bowl and mix well. Gradually add lime mixture and whisk to combine. Cover loosely with plastic wrap and refrigerate for 2–3 hours.

- Transfer chilled mixture to an ice cream maker and churn according to the manufacturer's instructions. Store in the freezer.

raspberry sorbet

Makes about 800 g (1¾ lb)

Raspberry purée *500 ml*
(16 fl oz / 2 cups)

Water *180 ml (6 fl oz / ¾ cup)*

Sugar *70 g (2½ oz)*

Inverted sugar syrup (trimoline)
1 Tbsp

Glucose powder *25 g (⅘ oz)*

- Combine raspberry purée and water in a mixing bowl. Mix well.

- Combine sugar, sugar syrup and glucose in a mixing bowl and mix well. Gradually add raspberry mixture and whisk to combine. Cover loosely with plastic wrap and refrigerate for 2–3 hours.

- Transfer chilled mixture to an ice cream maker and churn according to the manufacturer's instructions. Store in the freezer.

In glass: Lime Sorbet; Raspberry Sorbet

vanilla ice cream

Makes about 500 g (1 lb 1¹/₂ oz)

Vanilla bean *1, scraped for seeds and pod cut into 1-cm (¹/₂-in) lengths, or use 1 tsp vanilla essence*

Cream *125 ml (4 fl oz / ¹/₂ cup)*

Milk *220 ml (7²/₅ fl oz / ⁹/₁₀ cups)*

Egg yolks *65 g (2¹/₃ oz)*

Sugar *85 g (3 oz)*

- Combine vanilla seeds and pod or vanilla essence with cream and milk in a saucepan. Bring to the boil over low heat, then remove from heat.

- Whisk egg yolks and sugar in a mixing bowl. Stir in some warm milk mixture to temper egg yolks, then pour tempered mixture into saucepan and mix well with remaining milk mixture.

- Return saucepan to heat and bring mixture to 85°C (185°F), then place immediately into an ice bath to cool. Strain mixture into a bowl. Cover loosely with plastic wrap and refrigerate for 2–3 hours.

- Transfer chilled mixture to an ice cream maker and churn according to the manufacturer's instructions. Store in the freezer.

manjari ice cream

Makes about 540 g (1¹/₅ lb)

Milk *375 ml (12 fl oz / 1¹/₂ cups)*

Valrhona Manjari 64% chocolate *110 g (4 oz), chopped*

Sugar *30 g (1 oz)*

Skim milk *1¹/₄ Tbsp*

- Bring milk to the boil over low heat and stir in chocolate and sugar. Remove from heat and transfer to a bowl. Add skim milk and mix well, then leave to cool to room temperature.

- Cover loosely with plastic wrap and refrigerate for 2–3 hours.

- Transfer chilled mixture to an ice cream maker and churn according to the manufacturer's instructions. Store in the freezer.

From top: Vanilla Ice Cream, Manjari Ice Cream

green tea ice cream

Makes about 500 g (1 lb 1½ oz)

Cream *125 ml (4 fl oz / ½ cup)*
Milk *220 ml (7²/₅ fl oz / ⁹/₁₀ cups)*
Inverted sugar syrup (trimoline)
1 Tbsp
Egg yolks *55 g (2 oz)*
Sugar *55 g (2 oz)*
Glucose powder *15 g (½ oz)*
Green tea powder *10 g (⅓ oz)*

- Combine cream, milk and sugar syrup in a saucepan and bring to the boil. Remove from heat.

- Whisk egg yolks in a mixing bowl. Stir in some milk mixture to temper egg yolks, then mix well with remaining milk mixture.

- Combine sugar, glucose and green tea powders in another mixing bowl. Gradually add milk mixture and whisk to combine. Leave mixture to cool to room temperature.

- Cover loosely with plastic wrap and refrigerate for at 2–3 hours. Transfer chilled mixture to an ice cream maker and churn according to the manufacturer's instructions. Store in the freezer.

caramel ice cream

Makes about 900 g (1⁴/₅ lb)

Cream *60 ml
(2 fl oz / ¼ cup)*
Sugar *450 g (1 lb)*
Milk *300 ml (10 fl oz / 1¼ cups)*
Egg yolks *85 g (3 oz)*
Glucose powder *¾ Tbsp*

- Combine cream and milk in a saucepan and bring to the boil. Remove from heat and set aside to cool to 80°C (176°F).

- Meanwhile, caramelise 360 g (12²/₃ oz) sugar in a separate saucepan over low heat, until caramel is 180°C (350°F) and dark brown in colour. Remove from heat and gradually stir in milk mixture.

- Whisk egg yolks and glucose in a mixing bowl, then stir in some milk mixture to temper egg yolks. Add remaining milk mixture to mixing bowl and mix well. Leave to cool to room temperature.

- Cover loosely with plastic wrap and refrigerate for 2–3 hours. Transfer chilled mixture to an ice cream maker and churn according to the manufacturer's instructions. Store in the freezer.

strawberry ice cream

Makes about 540 g (1¹/₅ lb)

Cream *2 Tbsp*

Milk *150 ml (5¹/₃ fl oz / ³/₅ cup)*

Inverted sugar syrup (trimoline) *1¹/₄ Tbsp*

Sugar *55 g (2 oz)*

Milk powder *30 g (1 oz)*

Glucose powder *³/₄ Tbsp*

Strawberry purée *250 ml (8 fl oz / 1 cups)*

- Combine cream, milk and sugar syrup in a saucepan and bring to the boil. Remove from heat and set aside.

- Combine milk powder and glucose in a mixing bowl and mix well. Gradually add milk mixture and whisk to combine. Stir in strawberry purée and whisk to break up any lumps. Leave mixture to cool to room temperature.

- Cover loosely with plastic wrap and refrigerate for 2–3 hours. Transfer chilled mixture to an ice cream maker and churn according to the manufacturer's instructions. Store in the freezer.

From left: Green Tea Ice Cream, Caramel Ice Cream, Strawberry Ice Cream

black sesame ice cream

Makes about 500 g (1 lb 1¹/₂ oz)

Cream *125 ml (4 fl oz / ¹/₂ cup)*

Milk *200 ml (7 fl oz / ⁴/₅ cups)*

Egg yolks *55 g (2 oz)*

Sugar *70 g (2¹/₂ oz)*

Black sesame seed paste *60 ml (2 fl oz / ¹/₄ cup)*

- Combine cream and milk in a saucepan and bring to the boil. Remove from heat and set aside.

- Whisk egg yolks and sugar in a mixing bowl, then stir in some milk mixture to temper egg yolks. Pour tempered mixture into saucepan and mix well with remaining milk mixture.

- Stir in black sesame seed paste and heat mixture to 85°C (185°F). Remove from heat and immediately place into an ice bath to cool.

- Strain mixture into a bowl and cover loosely with plastic wrap. Refrigerate for 2–3 hours.

- Transfer chilled mixture to an ice cream maker and churn according to the manufacturer's instructions. Store in the freezer.

coffee ice cream

Makes about 900 g (1⁴/₅ lb)

Milk *635 ml (21 fl oz / 2³/₅ cups)*

Freshly ground coffee *1 tsp*

Egg yolks *30 g (1 oz)*

Sugar *125 g (4¹/₂ oz)*

Milk powder *45 g (1¹/₂ oz)*

Glucose powder *4 Tbsp*

Instant coffee granules *³/₄ Tbsp*

- Bring milk to the boil in a saucepan over low heat. Add ground coffee and stir to mix well. Remove from heat and leave aside for 1 hour. Strain mixture back into saucepan and set aside.

- Whisk egg yolks and sugar in a mixing bowl. Gradually add milk powder, glucose and coffee granules and whisk to combine. Stir in some milk mixture to temper egg yolks. Pour tempered mixture into saucepan and stir well with remaining milk mixture.

- Heat mixture to 85°C (185°F) and immediately place in an ice bath to cool. Strain into a bowl and cover loosely with plastic wrap. Refrigerate for 2–3 hours.

- Transfer chilled mixture to an ice cream maker and churn according to the manufacturer's instructions. Store in the freezer.

From left: Black Sesame Ice Cream, Coffee Ice Cream

cinnamon ice cream

Milk *220 ml (7²/₅ fl oz / ⁹/₁₀ cups)*

Cinnamon sticks *30 g (1 oz)*

Egg yolks *70 g (2¹/₂ oz)*

Cream *150 ml (5¹/₃ fl oz / ³/₅ cup)*

Sugar *85 g (3 oz)*

Makes about 540 g (1¹/₅ lb)

- Start preparations 1 day ahead.

- Pour milk into a mixing bowl. Break cinnamon sticks into pieces and add to milk. Cover and refrigerate overnight.

- Pour infused milk in a pot. Bring to the boil over low heat, stirring constantly. Strain milk into a mixing bowl.

- Whisk egg yolks, cream and sugar in another mixing bowl. Stir in some infused milk to temper egg yolks, then add remaining infused milk. Leave to cool to room temperature.

- Cover loosely with plastic wrap and refrigerate for 2–3 hours. Transfer chilled mixture to an ice cream maker and churn according to the manufacturer's instructions. Store in the freezer.

cream cheese ice cream

Makes about 1 kg (2 lb 3 oz)

Milk *500 ml (16 fl oz / 2 cups)*

Grated Parmesan cheese *30 g (1 oz)*

Cream cheese *125 g (4¹/₂ oz), diced*

Whipping cream *220 ml (7¹/₂ fl oz)*

Egg yolks *30 g (1 oz)*

Sugar *170 g (6 oz)*

ose powde   *¹/₂ oz)*

- Combine 180 ml (6 fl oz / ³/₄ cup) milk with Parmesan cheese in a saucepan over low heat and bring to the boil. Stir constantly to prevent cheese from burning. Gradually add cream cheese and stir until completely melted. Stir in cream and remove from heat.

- Strain milk mixture into a mixing bowl and stir in remaining milk. Set aside to cool.

- Whisk egg yolks, sugar and glucose powder in a mixing bowl. Stir in some milk mixture to temper egg yolks, then add remaining milk mixture. Leave to cool to room temperature.

- Cover loosely with plastic wrap and refrigerate for 2–3 hours. Transfer chilled mixture to an ice cream maker and churn according to the manufacturer's instructions. Store in the freezer.

chocolate 66% ice cream

Makes about 540 g (1¹/₅ lb)

Milk *375 ml (12 fl oz / 1¹/₂ cups)*

Valrhona Pur Caraibe 66% chocolate *110 g (4 oz), finely chopped*

Milk powder *20 g (²/₃ oz)*

Inverted sugar syrup (trimoline) *2 Tbsp*

Sugar *30 g (1 oz)*

- Bring milk to the boil over low heat and stir in chocolate, milk powder, sugar syrup and sugar. Remove from heat and transfer to a bowl. Leave to cool to room temperature.

- Cover loosely with plastic wrap and refrigerate for 2–3 hours. Transfer chilled mixture to an ice cream maker and churn according to the manufacturer's instructions. Store in the freezer.

{ dessert tapas }

Tapas are a variety of small Spanish savoury dishes which are commonly served at bars along with beer and other alcoholic beverages. Eschewing tradition in every way possible, the concept of tapas has been modified here to take the form of sweet confections that are dainty in size but big on taste. Give your guests a treat and serve up a combination of any of these dessert tapas at the end of a meal or at a tea party!

From left: Ice Cream with Hazelnut Rice Crispies, Banana Pizza, Chocolate Floating Island

ice cream with hazelnut rice crispies

Serves 3

Caramel ice cream (page 114)
3 scoops

Chocolate (66%) ice cream
(page 119) *3 scoops*

hazelnut chocolate rice puffs

Toasted rice puffs *20 g (²/₃ oz)*

Dark chocolate *45 g (1¹/₂ oz)*

Butter *5 g (¹/₆ oz)*

Hazelnut praline *45 g (1¹/₂ oz)*

- Prepare hazelnut chocolate rice puffs. Melt chocolate in a bain-marie. Remove from heat and stir in rice puffs. Mix well and set aside.

- Melt butter in a saucepan until lightly brown. Remove from heat and pour over praline in a bowl. Mix well, then add chocolate-coated rice puffs. Stir to mix evenly and set aside.

- Prepare 3 serving glasses. Place a scoop of caramel and chocolate ice cream into each glass and top with rice puffs. Serve immediately.

banana pizza

Makes 3

Puff pastry *9-cm (3.5-in)
square sheet*

Icing (confectioner's) sugar
for dusting

Bananas *2*

Sugar *70 g (2¹/₂ oz)*

Butter *25 g (⁴/₅ oz), softened*

Mascarpone cheese *35 g (1¹/₅ oz)*

Mozzarella cheese *55 g (2 oz),
grated*

Cinnamon sugar *15 g (¹/₅ oz)*

Cinnamon ice cream (page 118)
(optional)

- Preheat oven to 220°C (440°F).

- Place puff pastry on a baking tray and sprinkle icing sugar over. Bake for 8–10 minutes, then remove from heat and set aside to cool.

- Peel and cut bananas into 1-cm (¹/₂-in) thick slices and set aside. Caramelise sugar in a saucepan until dark brown. Add butter and stir until melted, then add bananas. Sauté for 3–5 minutes. Remove from heat and set aside to cool.

- Spread mascarpone cheese over puff pastry and top with mozzarella cheese. Sprinkle cinnamon sugar over and top with banana slices.

- Bake banana pizza in a preheated oven at 180°C (350°F) for 5–8 minutes until golden brown.

- Cut into 3 triangles and place onto 3 serving dishes. Top with ice cream, if desired and serve immediately.

chocolate floating island

Makes 5–6 servings

Passion fruit coulis (page 85)
1 quantity

chocolate sauce

Milk *250 ml (8 fl oz / 1 cup)*

Single (light) cream *100 ml (3¹/₂ fl oz / ²/₅ cup)*

Valrhona Manjari (64%) chocolate *130 g (4¹/₂ oz), finely chopped*

poached meringue

Egg whites *55 g (2 oz)*

Sugar *25 g (⁴/₅ oz)*

Salt *to taste*

- Prepare chocolate sauce. Combine milk and cream in a saucepan bring to a gentle simmer over low heat. Remove and set aside.

- Place chocolate in a mixing bowl and gently pour milk mixture over chocolate while stirring. Using a blender, blend mixture until smooth and set aside.

- Prepared poached meringue. Place egg whites in a mixing bowl and whisk on medium speed until foamy. Gradually add sugar and continue to whisk until light and fluffy, with firm peaks. Set aside.

- Place a pot of water over low heat. Add salt and bring to a gentle simmer. Make 10–12 quenelles from meringue using a tablespoon and poach for 5 minutes. Drain well and place on greaseproof paper.

- Warm chocolate sauce and pour into 5–6 serving glasses. Top each glass with 2 poached meringues and drizzle passion fruit coulis over. Serve immediately.

crème brûlée

Makes 8 servings

Vanilla bean *1/2, scraped for seeds,
or use 2 tsp vanilla essence*

Egg yolks *170 g (6 oz)*

Sugar *110 g (4 oz) + extra
for caramelising*

Single (light) cream *450 ml
(15 fl oz / 1⁴/₅ cups)*

Milk *85 ml (2¹/₂ fl oz / ¹/₃ cup)*

- Preheat oven to 95°C (203°F).

- Place vanilla seeds or essence, egg yolks and sugar in a mixing bowl and whisk to combine. Add cream and milk and mix well. Strain mixture.

- Pour mixture into eight 8-cm (3-in) wide and 4.5-cm (2-in) deep ramekins and bake for 1 hour. Remove from heat and set aside to cool to room temperature. Cover with plastic wrap and refrigerate for 1–2 hours until chilled and set.

- Sprinkle a thin layer of sugar over crème brûlée and caramelise with a blowtorch until light brown. Reheat crème brûlée in the microwave oven for 10–20 seconds on High and serve warm.

chocolate crème brûlée

Makes 8 servings

Milk *300 ml (10 fl oz / 1¹/₄ cups)*

Single (light) cream *125 ml
(4 fl oz / ¹/₂ cup)*

Sugar *45 g (1¹/₂ oz)*

Valrhona Pur Caraibe (66%)
chocolate *100 g (3¹/₂ oz),
finely chopped*

Egg yolks *70 g (2¹/₂ oz)*

- Preheat oven to 95°C (203°F).

- Combine milk, cream and sugar in a saucepan and bring to the boil. Remove from heat and set aside.

- Place chocolate in a mixing bowl and gently pour milk mixture over while stirring. Stir until chocolate is completely melted, then add egg yolks and whisk to combine.

- Pour mixture into eight 8-cm (3-in) wide and 4.5-cm (2-in) deep ramekins and bake for 45 minutes. Remove from heat and set aside to cool to room temperature. Cover with plastic wrap and refrigerate for 1–2 hours until chilled and set.

- Serve chilled, or reheat in the microwave oven for 10–20 seconds on High to serve warm. Garnish as desired.

From top: Crème Brûlée, Chocolate Crème Brûlée

From left: Strawberry Chocolate Fondue, Ginger Jelly, Hot Chocolate Shooter

strawberry chocolate fondue

Makes 5–7 servings

Valrhona Tropilia 53% chocolate *45 g (1¹/₂ oz), chopped*

Single (light) cream *2 Tbsp*

Strawberries *350 g (12¹/₃ oz), cleaned and hulled*

Mint leaves

sugar syrup

Sugar *100 g (3¹/₂ oz)*

Water *3¹/₂ Tbsp*

- Prepare sugar syrup. Combine sugar and water and bring to the boil over low heat. Stir until sugar is completely dissolved, then remove from heat. Set aside to cool. This recipe requires only 3–4 Tbsp syrup. Store remaining syrup in an airtight container and keep refrigerated for up to 2 weeks.

- Place chocolate in a mixing bowl and set aside. Combine sugar syrup and cream in a saucepan and heat to 85°C (185°F). Remove from heat and gently pour over chocolate while stirring. Stir until chocolate is completely melted. Mix well.

- Warm chocolate sauce over low heat for 1–2 minutes. Divide strawberries into 5–7 serving glasses and drizzle chocolate sauce over. Garnish with mint leaves and serve immediately.

ginger jelly

Makes about 10 servings

Water *500 ml (16 fl oz / 2 cups)*

Ginger tea leaves *6 g (^{1}/$_5$ oz)*

Agar agar powder *^{1}/$_2$ g (^{1}/$_{20}$ oz)*

Sugar *500 g (1 lb 1^1/$_2$ oz)*

Gelatine sheet *^{1}/$_2$ g (^{1}/$_{20}$ oz), soaked in ice water to soften and drained*

Canned lychees *10*

Ginger *55 g (2 oz), peeled and sliced*

- Start preparations 1 day ahead.

- Bring water to the boil and add tea to infuse. Set aside to cool, then refrigerate overnight.

- Strain tea into a pot and bring to the boil over low heat. Add agar agar powder, sugar and softened gelatine and stir until ingredients are completely dissolved. Remove from heat and set aside to cool. Pour jelly mixture into 10 serving glasses. Refrigerate for 2–3 hours until set.

- Cut lychees into small pieces and place in a bowl. Add ginger and cover with plastic wrap. Refrigerate for 1 hour for flavours to infuse.

- Spoon lychees onto jellies and serve chilled.

hot chocolate shooter

Makes 15 servings

Vanilla ice cream (page 113) *250 ml (8 fl oz / 1 cup)*

chocolate sauce

Milk *400 ml (13^1/$_2$ fl oz / 1^3/$_5$ cups)*

Single (light) cream *150 ml (5^1/$_3$ fl oz / ^{3}/$_5$ cups)*

Valrhona Pur Caraibe 66% chocolate *100 g (3^1/$_2$ oz), chopped*

Valrhona Tropilia 53% chocolate *100 g (3^1/$_2$ oz), chopped*

- Prepare chocolate sauce. Combine milk and cream in a saucepan and bring to a simmer over low heat. Remove from heat and set aside.

- Place chocolates in a mixing bowl and gently pour milk mixture over while stirring. Transfer mixture to a blender and blend until smooth. Pour chocolate sauce into 15 shot glasses.

- Top chocolate sauce with ice cream. Garnish as desired and serve immediately.

From left: Lemon Posset, Crème Chamomile, Lychee Foam

lemon posset

Makes 5–7 servings

Single (light) cream *220 ml*
(7²/₅ fl oz / ⁹/₁₀ cup)
Milk *220 ml (7²/₅ fl oz / ⁹/₁₀ cup)*
Sugar *110 g (4 oz)*
Lemon juice *85 ml*
(2¹/₂ fl oz / ¹/₃ cup)

blueberry compote
Frozen blueberries *110 g (4 oz)*
Sugar *35 g (1¹/₅ oz)*
Vanilla essence *1 tsp*

- Combine cream, milk and sugar in a saucepan and bring to the boil. Remove from heat and set aside to cool slightly.

- Add lemon juice to milk mixture. Stir to mix, then divide into 5–7 small glasses. Refrigerate, uncovered, for 6 hours until chilled and set.

- About 2 hours before lemon posset is ready, prepare blueberry compote. Preheat oven to 150°C (300°F).

- Combine all ingredients in a mixing bowl and mix well. Transfer to an ovenproof dish and bake for 1 hour. Remove from heat and set aside to cool. Refrigerate for 1 hour until chilled.

- Spoon 1–2 Tbsp blueberry compote over lemon possets, then serve chilled.

lychee foam

Makes 20 servings

Single (light) cream *300 ml*
(10 fl oz / 1¹/₄ cups)
Gelatine sheets *10 g (¹/₃ oz),*
soaked in ice water to soften
and drained
Lychee purée *500 ml*
(16 fl oz / 2 cups)
Kirsch liqueur (Kirschwasser)
2¹/₄ Tbsp
Lychees *for garnishing*

- Pour cream into a saucepan and bring to the boil. Stir in softened gelatine, lychee purée and liqueur. Stir until gelatine is completely dissolved.

- Pour mixture into a whipped cream cylinder with a gas capsule and use according to the manufacturer's instructions. Refrigerate for 2 hours until chilled.

- Pipe foam into prepared serving glasses and garnish with lychees. Serve chilled.

crème chamomile

Chamomile tea bags *10 g (¹/₃ oz)*

Single (light) cream *375 ml (12 fl oz / 1¹/₂ cups)*

Sugar *40 g (1¹/₂ oz)*

Gelatine sheet

Water for gelatine *1 Tbsp*

sugar work (optional)

Isomalt *100 g (3¹/₂ oz)*

Pink food colouring

Makes 4 servings

- Start preparations 1 day in ahead.

- Place tea bags in cream and leave to infuse in the refrigerator overnight.

- Soak gelatine in water to soften and set aside. Strain cream into a saucepan. Add sugar and bring to the boil, stirring constantly until sugar is completely dissolved. Add softened gelatine and water and stir until completely dissolved. Remove from heat and set aside to cool.

- Pour mixture into 4 serving glasses. Cover with plastic wrap and refrigerate for 1–2 hours until chilled and set. Crème chamomile will keep refrigerated for up to 5 days.

- Prepare sugar work, if desired. Combine isomalt and colouring in a small mixing bowl and mix well. Spread isomalt on a silicone mat. Place another silicone mat on top and bake in a preheated oven at 180°C (350°F) for 2–3 minutes or until sugar is melted. Remove from heat and leave sugar sandwiched between silicone mats until cooled and hardened. Remove silicone mat and cut sugar into desired shapes.

- Garnish crème chamomile with sugar work and serve chilled.

orange confit

kirsch liqueur

yeast

rye flour

chocolate chips

mascarpone cheese

dark chocolate

white chocolate

cake flour

paillete feuilletine

gold flakes

vanilla bean

gelatine

{ glossary }

Chocolate Chips These small, round discs of chocolate are popularly used in baking, as they are manufactured to retain their shape due to a low content of cocoa butter (edible vegetable fat that can be found in chocolate). Chocolate chips can also be melted and used in sauces.

Chocolate, Dark Dark chocolate comes in varieties of sweet and bittersweet (semi-sweet) flavours. Sweetened dark chocolate contains a high amount of sugar and a lower amount of chocolate liquor, whereas bittersweet dark chocolate has relatively equal amounts of sugar and chocolate liquor. Dark chocolate may also contain flavouring additives. Unsweetened dark chocolate is also available and is suitable for baking and cooking.

Chocolate, White Unlike milk or dark chocolate, white chocolate does not contain chocolate liquor or cocoa solids. It is made of sugar, milk solids, vegetable fats and cocoa butter, and has a lower melting point as compared to dark chocolate. White chocolate is ivory coloured, with a sweet, creamy taste.

Flour, Rye Rye flour has a low gluten content and is used to produce sticky, dense breads. It can be combined with wheat flour to make lighter breads. Breads made with rye flours are able to retain their moisture longer than breads made purely of wheat flour.

Flour, Cake Cake flour is a variety of wheat flour that has a low gluten content. It produces a ligher, finer crumb in cakes, with a less chewy texture.

Gelatine Sold in sheets or in powder form, gelatine is a colourless, translucent substance made from animal protein. It behaves as a thickening agent when added to liquids, causing the liquid to gel. Store in an airtight container in a cool, dry place.

Gold Leaf Gold leaf is made from gold that is beaten into extremely thin sheets and treated, so it is edible, although it has no perceivable smell or taste. Used to decorate baked goods, gold leaves are also available in flake or powdered form.

Kirsch Liqueur Also known as Kirschwasser in German, this is a brandy made from fermenting sweet or sour cherries. In its pure form, kirsch liqueur is colourless and unsweetened, with a subtle taste of cherries. It can be consumed as an apéritif, used as part of a cocktail mixture, or used to flavour jellies and puddings.

Mascarpone Cheese Mascarpone is a thick, creamy cheese traditionally made by curdling milk, then blending it with tartaric acid to create its dense texture. Mascarpone is white in colour and has a creamy, milky flavour. It is most commonly used in making tiramisu.

Orange Confit Orange confit is available in baking supply stores. This preserved orange peel retains its colour and form despite undergoing a process of candying and drying. It is made by blanching fresh orange peel several times to remove its bitterness, then removing the white pith on the underside. The prepared peel is soaked in a hot sugar syrup for a few hours, before it is drained and coated with sugar and placed in a moderately warm oven to dry.

Paillete Feuilletine

These crushed, thin wafer flakes are available in professional baking stores. They serve to add a crunchy texture to pralines, cake bases and chocolate confections.

Vanilla Bean Vanilla beans contain tiny black seeds that are highly aromatic. To extract a stronger flavour from the bean, especially when used in pastry creams, split the bean in two, scrape the seeds out and add both the pod and seeds to the cream. Substitute with vanilla essence if the beans are not available.

Yeast Yeast is a microscopic fungus used for leavening baked goods. Through the process of fermentation, yeast produces carbon dioxide, which causes the dough to rise and expand, giving the baked product a light, springy texture. Yeast is available fresh or dry, as well as in instant form. Fresh yeast is highly perishable and should be used quickly upon purchase. Dry yeast needs to be combined with warm water to rehydrate it. Instant yeast does not require warm water for rehydration and can be blended directly with flour. . Dry and instant yeast have a much longer shelf life as compared to fresh yeast. If unopened, both forms can keep up to a year in a cool, dry place. Upon opening, dry and instant yeast should be refrigerated and can keep for up to 6 months.

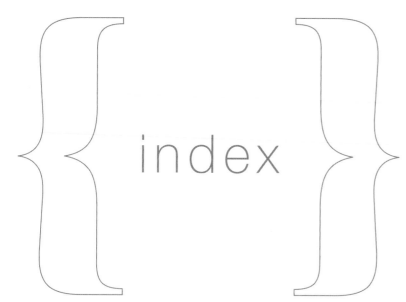

{ index }

weights and measures

Quantities for this book are given in Metric and American (spoon and cup) measures. Standard spoon and cup measurements used are: 1 teaspoon = 5 ml, 1 tablespoon = 15 ml, 1 cup = 250 ml. All measures are level unless otherwise stated.

LIQUID AND VOLUME MEASURES

Metric	Imperial	American
5 ml	1/6 fl oz	1 teaspoon
10 ml	1/3 fl oz	1 dessertspoon
15 ml	1/2 fl oz	1 tablespoon
60 ml	2 fl oz	1/4 cup (4 tablespoons)
85 ml	2 1/2 fl oz	1/3 cup
90 ml	3 fl oz	3/8 cup (6 tablespoons)
125 ml	4 fl oz	1/2 cup
180 ml	6 fl oz	3/4 cup
250 ml	8 fl oz	1 cup
300 ml	10 fl oz (1/2 pint)	1 1/4 cups
375 ml	12 fl oz	1 1/2 cups
435 ml	14 fl oz	1 3/4 cups
500 ml	16 fl oz	2 cups
625 ml	20 fl oz (1 pint)	2 1/2 cups
750 ml	24 fl oz (1 1/5 pints)	3 cups
1 litre	32 fl oz (1 3/5 pints)	4 cups
1.25 litres	40 fl oz (2 pints)	5 cups
1.5 litres	48 fl oz (2 2/5 pints)	6 cups
2.5 litres	80 fl oz (4 pints)	10 cups

DRY MEASURES

Metric	Imperial
30 grams	1 ounce
45 grams	1 1/2 ounces
55 grams	2 ounces
70 grams	2 1/2 ounces
85 grams	3 ounces
100 grams	3 1/2 ounces
110 grams	4 ounces
125 grams	4 1/2 ounces
140 grams	5 ounces
280 grams	10 ounces
450 grams	16 ounces (1 pound)
500 grams	1 pound, 1 1/2 ounces
700 grams	1 1/2 pounds
800 grams	1 3/4 pounds
1 kilogram	2 pounds, 3 ounces
1.5 kilograms	3 pounds, 4 1/2 ounces
2 kilograms	4 pounds, 6 ounces

OVEN TEMPERATURE

	°C	°F	Gas Regulo
Very slow	120	250	1
Slow	150	300	2
Moderately slow	160	325	3
Moderate	180	350	4
Moderately hot	190/200	370/400	5/6
Hot	210/220	410/440	6/7
Very hot	230	450	8
Super hot	250/290	475/550	9/10

LENGTH

Metric	Imperial
0.5 cm	1/4 inch
1 cm	1/2 inch
1.5 cm	3/4 inch
2.5 cm	1 inch

Be patient and practise a lot. Throw in a good dose of passion and you're on your way to perfecting your baking skills.